ROYAL PALACES

WINDSOR
CASTLE

H.M. THE QUEEN AND H.R.H. THE
DUKE OF EDINBURGH RETURNING
IN AN OPEN CARRIAGE after the
Garter Service in St George's
Chapel on 13 June 1994.

ROYAL PALACES

WINDSOR CASTLE

A Short History

A Royal Collection Book

Published by Michael Joseph Limited
in association with Royal Collection Enterprises Limited

Penguin Books Limited
27 Wrights Lane, London W8 5TZ
Viking Penguin Inc., 375 Hudson Street, New York, New York 10014, USA
Penguin Books Australia Ltd, Ringwood, Victoria, Australia
Penguin Books Canada Ltd, 10 Alcorn Avenue, Toronto, Ontario, Canada M4V 3B2
Penguin Books (NZ) Ltd, 182-190 Wairau Road, Auckland 10, New Zealand

Penguin Books, Registered Offices: Harmondsworth, Middlesex, England

First published 1996
Text written by John Martin Robinson
Copyright © Royal Collection Enterprises Limited 1996

Illustrations:
All photographs copyright © Her Majesty The Queen

Colour reproduction by Radstock Reproductions Limited
Printed in Great Britain by Butler & Tanner Ltd, Frome and London

A CIP catalogue record for this book is available from the British Library
ISBN 0 7181 3969 0
1 3 5 7 9 10 8 6 4 2

CONTENTS

INTRODUCTION

(*Left*) THE LOWER WARD WITH THE
PROCESSION OF THE KNIGHTS OF
THE GARTER TO THEIR ANNUAL
SERVICE IN ST GEORGE'S CHAPEL.
The Garter ceremonies including
the investment of new knights, a feast
and choral service in St George's
Chapel used to be held on St
George's Day in April but now take
place in June.

Windsor Castle is one of the most important secular historic buildings in Britain. It is the largest inhabited castle in the world and the longest-occupied royal palace in Europe; it is comparable with the Vatican, the Escorial or Versailles in its fame and national associations. It is an architectural epitome of the history of the English nation, and its skyline of battlements, turrets and the great Round Tower is instantly recognizable throughout the world.

Windsor Castle is more like a fortified town than a house. It covers over thirteen acres. It includes a large collegiate church, homes for scores of people from the Constable and Governor of the Castle and the Military Knights of Windsor and their families to the Dean, Canons and choristers of St George's Chapel, and a guard which is frequently formed from a battalion of one of the Household Regiments. And it is a royal palace where the court is in residence in April and June every year, and where The Queen spends most of her private weekends.

St George's Chapel is, with King's College Chapel, Cambridge, and Henry VII's Chapel, Westminster, one of the supreme achievements of English late medieval Gothic. The Upper Ward, as remodelled by Charles II and George IV, forms a truly splendid palace; one, moreover, which still retains an incomparable collection of works of art, some still displayed in the rooms for which they were specially commissioned or collected. This book explains how the Castle developed through the centuries, and how the collection of works of art was assembled.

Geometricall Paſes, of 5 Feet,

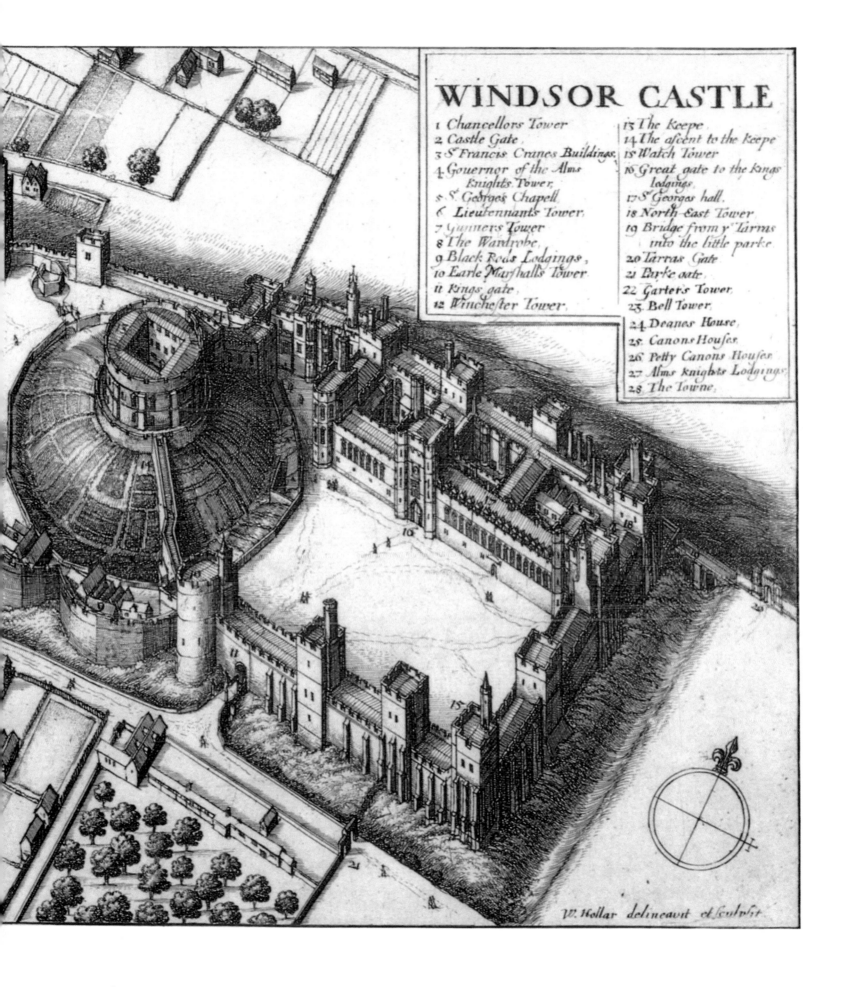

WINDSOR CASTLE

1. Chancellors Tower
2. Castle Gate
3. S.t Francis Cranes Buildings.
4. Gouernor of the Alms Knights Tower.
5. S.t Georges Chapell
6. Lieutenants Tower
7. Gunners Tower
8. The Wardrobe
9. Black Rods Lodgings,
10. Earle Marshalls Tower
11. Kings gate
12. Winchester Tower.

13. The Keepe
14. The ascent to the Keepe
15. Watch Tower
16. Great gate to the Kings lodgings.
17. S.t Georges hall.
18. North East Tower
19. Bridge from y.e Tarras into the little parke.
20. Tarras Gate
21. Parke gate
22. Garters Tower
23. Bell Tower

24. Deanes House,
25. Canons Houses.
26. Petty Canons Houses
27. Alms knights Lodgings.
28. The Towne.

W. Hollar delineavit et sculpsit

CHAPTER ONE

THE MIDDLE AGES

Creation of the Castle

The exact date of Windsor's foundation is not known. It was one of a chain of castles established as a defensive ring by William the Conqueror in the 1070s and 1080s to protect London, following his subjugation of England: Berkhamsted, Hertford, Ongar and Rayleigh to the north; Rochester, Tonbridge, Reigate and Guildford to the south; with Windsor guarding the Thames to the west. It occupies the only naturally defensive site in this part of the Thames Valley, a chalk ridge 100 ft (30.5 m) above the river bank, forming a detached outcrop of the Chiltern Hills.

Norman castles were often built to a standard plan, with an artificial earthen mound (motte) supporting a tower or keep of timber or stone, the entrance to which was protected by an outer fenced courtyard (bailey) – hence the description of this type of layout as a motte-and-bailey castle.

Windsor is the most notable example of a particularly distinctive version of this basic plan, developed for use on a ridge site. It comprises a central motte with a large bailey to either side of it (known at Windsor as the Lower and Upper Wards), rather than just on one side as was more usual. It is not a unique plan, however: Arundel Castle in Sussex, Rockingham Castle in Northamptonshire and Alnwick Castle in Northumberland all originally had similar plans, and there are other examples in William's native Normandy, such as the Château of Grimboscai near Caen.

The Norman and Angevin kings were constantly on the move, riding from manor to manor and castle to castle in Normandy, Anjou and England, in order to satisfy the needs of justice and administration, as well as for hunting and recreation. During the Middle Ages the Royal Household was the government of the country

VIEW OF WINDSOR CASTLE FROM THE RIVER THAMES. The skyline of battlements and turrets dominated by the great Round Tower is instantly recognizable throughout the world. The chalk ridge 100 ft (30m) above the river formed a perfect defensive site for the Castle.

and much of it travelled with the King, only a few institutions such as the Treasury staying in one place. This restless existence made the King's presence felt all over his territories and was an important aspect of royal policy. Over the years a certain pattern developed in these regal progresses. Thus Christmas and the great feasts of the year came to be spent in particular places. William the Conqueror, when he was in England, wore his crown three times a year – in Winchester at Easter, in Westminster at Whitsuntide and in Gloucester at Christmas. On these great formal or 'state' occasions he entertained all the great men of the realm: earls, thanes and knights, archbishops, bishops and abbots. The annual state opening of Parliament at Westminster is a survival of this ancient custom into modern times.

In addition to these principal palaces, with their great halls, which formed the setting for the ceremonial occasions when the King appeared in state surrounded by his barons, the King possessed a large number of more private castles and hunting lodges where he spent some of his time and which offered him sport in surrounding forests as relaxation from the business of government. The Normans introduced deer hunting into England, initially as a royal sport. Windsor began its present role as a royal residence in the guise of a hunting lodge.

As first built, the Castle had been entirely defensive, constructed of earth and timber, but easy access from London and the proximity of the Castle to the old royal hunting forest of the Saxon kings, immediately to the south (of which part was later enclosed as Windsor Great Park), soon recommended it as a royal residence. Henry I is known to have had domestic quarters in the Castle as early as 1110 and his son, Henry II, converted the Castle into a palace. He built two separate sets of royal apartments within the fortified enclosure: a public or official state residence in the Lower Ward, with a Great Hall where he could entertain his court and the barons on state occasions, and a smaller private residence on the north side of the Upper Ward for his own exclusive occupation. Thus he ingeniously combined both types of royal residence in a single, albeit large, curtilage.

Henry II, the greatest of the Angevin kings, was a lavish builder at all his residences. The Abbot of Mont St Michel wrote in 1161: 'not only in Normandy but also in England, in the Duchy of Aquitaine, in the County of Anjou, in Maine and Touraine, he either repaired old castles and palaces or built new ones.' Castle building under Henry

THE ROUND TOWER FROM THE UPPER WARD. The earthen motte was constructed by William the Conqueror, and the circular stone keep begun by Henry II. The upper 30 feet (9 m) and the battlements were added by Jeffry Wyatville for George IV, to improve the skyline.

II, as under his successors Richard I and King John, was the largest single item of royal expenditure. The aim of much of this work was not to strengthen the defences of the royal castles but to improve their domestic amenities. As well as Windsor, Henry II converted Winchester Castle into a palace, and built spacious unfortified houses at Clarendon, Wiltshire, and Woodstock, Oxfordshire, and improved the accommodation within the fortifications of many of the royal castles in the Midlands and in the south of England.

The stone for the new residential buildings constructed at Windsor in 1165-71 was brought from Bedfordshire. Henry II also began to replace the old timber outer walls of the Upper Ward with stone, using a hard heath stone found ten miles south of Windsor at Bagshot. The basic curtain wall round the Upper Ward, much modified by later alterations and improvements, dates from Henry II's time, as does the old part of the stone keep, known as the Round Tower, on top of William the Conqueror's motte. The reconstruction of the curtain wall round the Lower Ward was completed over the next sixty years, the well-preserved section visible from the High Street with its three half-round towers being built by Henry III. His predecessor King John's work on the fortifications was interrupted when in 1215 he was besieged by the barons who forced him to sign Magna Carta at Runnymede, the flat field beside the Thames near Windsor where they were based.

Henry III, who came of age in 1227 and married Eleanor of Provence in 1236, was the greatest builder among the English medieval kings. Architecture was his chief passion and Westminster Abbey is his most complete surviving monument. He took a keen personal interest

THE LOWER WARD SHOWING THE CURTAIN WALL AND CURFEW TOWER. This part of the outer defences was constructed by Henry III in the first half of the thirteenth century. The windows and the French-looking candle-snuffer roof of the tower were added in the nineteenth century by Anthony Salvin.

in all his projects: for instance, he sent detailed architectural instructions to the builders in England when he was in France. Wherever he was, his clerks were called to take down his instructions, which read more like architectural specifications than ordinary government documents. Henry III carried out extensive works at Windsor, spending more money there than at any of his other major houses. In his time it became one of the three principal royal palaces alongside Westminster and Winchester. He completely rebuilt Henry II's buildings in the Lower Ward and added there a large new Chapel, all forming a coherently planned layout round a courtyard with a cloister. Parts of Henry III's buildings survive embedded in later structures in the Lower Ward. He also further improved the royal private apartments in the Upper Ward, as well as completing the circuit of stone walls round the Lower Ward. His work on the private apartments in the Upper Ward included a new Hall on the ground floor, the upper part of which is now occupied by the Grand Reception Room. The compact plan of Henry III's quadrangular buildings forming the 'official' palace in the Lower Ward was dictated by the constricted space within the Castle and contrasts with the more spreading, somewhat incoherent, plans of most medieval domestic buildings. Henry III devised two complete sets of grand new rooms for himself and his queen; these included two chapels.

The King's Chapel at Windsor was the most imposing of the many private chapels which Henry III built for himself; he had no fewer than fifty chapels in his different houses. That at Windsor was later destroyed, probably in the reign of Henry VII without being recorded, but it is known to have had a timber vault painted to look like stone. The west doors, with magnificent ironwork signed by the blacksmith Gilebertus, alone survive at the east end of St George's Chapel behind the high altar, and give an indication of the quality of all that has been lost. The Chapel was 70 ft (21.3 m) long and 28 ft (8.5 m) wide and must have been comparable in scale and richness with the Sainte Chapelle in Paris, built by his cousin, Louis IX.

Henry III visited Paris for the first time only in 1254 and it was the Sainte Chapelle which he most wanted to see while he was there. A contemporary poem imaginatively quotes him as declaring that, if he could, he would like to bring it home with him in a cart. As the Windsor Chapel was already completed by then, the Sainte Chapelle can have had no first-hand influence on its design, though the King's Paris visit did have significant impact on the design of Westminster Abbey.

Even less is known about the Queen's Chapel at Windsor than the King's, except that it was two-storeyed, with the Queen's pew situated in the upper gallery or tribune entered directly from her apartments, while her household sat down below in the body of the building. Henry and his queen were both very pious. The King went to Mass three times a day, which even Louis IX thought excessive.

The chapels and the new royal rooms at Windsor were elaborately decorated, as were the interiors of all Henry III's houses, with stained glass in the windows, carved wood ceilings, richly tiled floors (like

JORIS HOEFNAGEL: engraving of Windsor Castle from the north in the reign of Elizabeth I.

that which can still be seen in the chapter house of Westminster Abbey) and wall paintings. These murals were of biblical and other religious themes, historical subjects or even great contemporary events, such as the crusades in the Holy Land. The Queen's Chamber, for instance, had its walls painted with the Tree of Jesse, and the ceiling was painted green with gold stars. The vivid colouring which distinguished Henry III's architecture is recalled in the restored scarlet gesso and gilded ironwork of his chapel doors. The King himself specified the subjects for the painters to execute. The names of some of the artists who worked for him are recorded in the account rolls, including Master William of Westminster (a Benedictine monk), Master Walter of Durham (a layman) and the latter's son Thomas. Their workmanship was of 'the highest technical excellence' and was one of the high-water marks of English medieval art. Only small fragments survive, but some idea of their original impact can be gathered from the rolls of accounts and records.

Henry III's substantial programme at Windsor was totally eclipsed a hundred years later by Edward III in the 1350s, 1360s and 1370s. Edward III's work at Windsor was not only the most important

ST GEORGE'S CHAPEL: door at the east end of the present Chapel. This survives from Henry III's original chapel. The ironwork is signed by the smith Gilebertus, and gives an idea of the high artistic quality of Henry III's work at Windsor.

palace-building project of the later Middle Ages, but the most ambitious single architectural scheme in the whole history of the English royal residences. His transformation of the Castle into a vast Gothic palace, redolent of the medieval ideals of Christian chivalry, determines Windsor's character even today. Edward III's building work was paid for out of the proceeds of the King's successful wars in France, and celebrated his military triumphs there. The major burst of activity took place in the 1350s, following the crushing defeats of the French at Crécy and Poitiers, the capture of Calais (which remained an English possession for two hundred years), and the imposition of independent English sovereignty over Aquitaine and Gascony, which had formerly been held as fiefs from the French crown, at least in name.

At Windsor Edward III spent more on converting the Castle into a splendid fortified palace than any other medieval English king spent on any other single building. Windsor was the intended centre of his court and government, and the seat of the newly founded Order of the Garter. It expressed Edward III's conception of kingship as surely as Versailles did that of Louis XIV or the Vatican that of the papacy. It was a statement of strong personal monarchy and military glory. As he grew older – and he reigned for over fifty years, longer almost than any other medieval king – Edward spent less time at Westminster and more at Windsor; the hunting lodge which Henry III had built in Windsor Great Park became Edward's favourite retreat from the cares of state, rather in the way that, five hundred years later, Osborne House on the Isle of Wight was to be Queen Victoria's. After 1372 the chief officers of the household were based permanently at Windsor. When the King moved to his lesser houses, he was accompanied no longer by his full household, as in the early Middle Ages, but just by his personal attendants, forming a smaller 'riding household'; and this pattern survived for the remainder of the medieval period.

Edward III's work at Windsor, which began in 1350, falls into two phases: work in the Lower Ward consequent on the founding of the Order of the Garter, and work in the Upper Ward, where a new palace was constructed round three courts on the north side of the Quadrangle.

The alterations to the Lower Ward were designed to provide accommodation for the priestly College of St George, founded on 6 August 1348 as the religious complement of the Order of the Garter. It comprised a Dean, twelve Canons and thirteen

Vicars-choral. In addition, there were to be twenty-six Poor Knights, who were to attend Mass daily as a substitute for the Companions of the Order who were too busy elsewhere. Henry III's handsome Chapel was made over to the Order and renamed St George's Chapel. Henry's royal lodgings in the Lower Ward were transformed into accommodation for the clergy and a new cloister was built, with traceried Perpendicular windows and a massive beamed ceiling, as well as a treasury and chapter house. A mechanical weight-driven clock, the earliest recorded in England, was set up in the Round Tower at the same time. These various works, which cost £6,500, were completed by 1358, and to mark the occasion the Feast of St George was celebrated by the King and court with great splendour at the Castle that year.

The reconstruction of the Upper Ward, begun in 1357, was on a larger scale than the work in the Lower Ward. The new royal lodgings were constructed of stone, initially under the direction of William of Wykeham, Surveyor of the King's Works and later Bishop of Winchester. An inner gatehouse, flanked by two cylindrical towers, was built to give access to the Upper Ward from the Lower in 1359. It still survives, albeit restored, but is now misleadingly called the Norman Gateway. Only some of the masonry of the present State

THE NORMAN GATEWAY. This is not in fact Norman, but was built by Edward III in 1357 as the principal entrance to his new palace in the Upper Ward. The tower on the left was restored by Jeffry Wyatville

Apartments and the handsome vaulted undercroft survives of Edward III's royal lodgings, but the original accounts, together with the engravings of Windsor by Wenceslas Hollar in Elias Ashmole's seventeenth-century *History of the Most Noble Order of the Garter* and recent archaeological discoveries, give some impression. The major new apartments were on the first floor and consisted of separate sets of rooms for the King and the Queen, in accordance with the traditional arrangement of the English royal residences; they were raised over vaulted undercrofts, the stone ribbed ceilings of which were supported on slender octagonal piers and remain in the Grand Entrance and Servants' Hall. The principal rooms were grouped around two courtyards, later known as the Brick Court and the Horn Court, with two-tier cloisters and paving of Purbeck marble.

The King's apartment consisted of five chambers and a closet, as

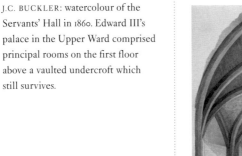

J.C. BUCKLER: watercolour of the Servants' Hall in 1860. Edward III's palace in the Upper Ward comprised principal rooms on the first floor above a vaulted undercroft which still survives.

did the Queen's. The other principal rooms included a Great Chamber on the site of the Grand Reception Room and a Painted Chamber. To the east, flanking a smaller courtyard, was a large new kitchen and other offices, including a well 10 ft (3 m) in diameter and 130 ft (39.6 m) deep. Along the south side, facing into the Quadrangle of the Upper Ward, were the Great Hall and Private Chapel, end to end – an identical arrangement to that still surviving at William of Wykeham's New College, Oxford.

By his death in 1377, Edward III had spent £50,772 on Windsor Castle. But of his work, the only parts which survive as visually coherent pieces of architecture are the cloisters of St George's Chapel, the Norman Gateway and the undercroft of the State Apartments. Everything else was disguised and altered in the reconstructions of the seventeenth and nineteenth centuries. The existing St George's Hall, for example, comprises the space of both

Edward III's Chapel and Hall knocked together in the early nineteenth century; and the King's and Queen's State Apartments were
completely remodelled and redecorated in the seventeenth, eighteenth and nineteenth centuries.

PAUL SANDBY: view through the
Norman Gate, in the reign of
George III, looking westwards
towards the Winchester Tower.
Edward III's stone vault survives.

Enough is known, however, about the appearance of Edward III's
new palace in the Upper Ward at Windsor to be able to see that it
was of considerable architectural interest and originality. It was also
an important source of influence on a number of other medieval
buildings. Edward III's aim was to create one large palace which
contained both the State Apartments for official and ceremonial
business, and the King's and Queen's own private apartments, in a
single unified residence.

The new buildings had several unusual architectural features.
The most striking was that all the principal apartments, including
the Hall and Chapel, were on the same level, raised up on the *piano
nobile*. This was quite different from the other medieval royal
palaces, like Westminster and Clarendon, where many of the principal rooms, including the hall, were situated on the ground floor.
The rooms at Windsor must have been approached by a large flight

of stone steps, perhaps in one of the three internal courtyards, though the exact location is not known.

Another novel feature of the design was the attempt to create a symmetrical south façade to the Quadrangle in the Upper Ward. The eighteen bays of the Hall and Chapel were given identical tall traceried windows, and were flanked at either end by a matching pair of gatehouses, one on the site of the present Grand Entrance forming the principal entry, and the other leading to the kitchen court and later called the Kitchen Gate, though this may not have been its original function as it seems odd to have given the same architectural significance to the kitchen entrance as to the royal entrance.

Both these new gatehouses were treated in a mock military manner, with a central archway, machicolations, battlements and flanking polygonal turrets which rose a storey higher than the adjoining two-storeyed domestic ranges. These gatehouses cannot, despite their machicolations, battlements and turrets, have been intended to serve a defensive purpose, as the intervening walls were punctuated with large, indefensible, glazed windows. They must therefore have been a deliberate attempt to deploy a military aesthetic for architectural effect. As such, they were the earliest examples of this genre in English architecture, and predate the late medieval castle houses, such as Herstmonceux in Sussex, by a hundred years. They perfectly reflected Edward III's cult of military chivalry, and they parallel the work on the Continent of the Duke of Burgundy and the Duc de Berri (whose extraordinary decorative Gothic houses and castles are recorded in the illuminated miniatures of his *Très Riches Heures* at Chantilly). Unlike the Duc de Berri's buildings, however, with their lavish external carving, colouring and gilding, Edward III's Windsor was more restrained, more severe and thus very English.

Little is known about the interior of Edward III's principal storey at Windsor, though a circular stone ribbed vault with a carved central boss and the remains of painted murals survive in the little La Rose tower at the west end of the south front. The names of the rooms are known from the inventories, though not their exact disposition. They all seem to have been remarkably uniform, however. They were all of the same height, with similar tall traceried windows, and similar low-pitched timber ceilings with chamfered and moulded beams. The latter formed a distinctive 'Windsor-School' design and can still be seen in the roof over the Hall built by Edward III next to Henry II's Round Tower. The

J. STEPHANOFF: watercolour of the Kitchen in the Upper Ward in the reign of George III. Built by Edward III, this great medieval space has remained in constant use. The roof is actually of timber and the old beams survived the fire of 1992.

fourteenth-century roof of the Great Kitchen also survives, and is a variation on the same theme (the beams were later encased by Wyatville). Another of Edward III's timber roofs, though not now visible, survives above Wyatville's plaster ceiling of the Garter Throne Room; and the woodwork from others was reused, in the seventeenth century, to make the floor structure of what is now the Grand Reception Room. All these timber structures help to give an impression of what Edward III's rooms must have looked like. The walls were mainly plastered and painted, though there is evidence from the careful choice and treatment of different colours of stonework in certain areas that some of the spaces were lined with unplastered ashlar masonry.

The Hall and Chapel were on a larger scale than the other rooms. They also differed in size from the Hugh May interiors which succeeded them in the seventeenth century. In Edward III's time the Hall was larger and the Chapel smaller, and both were lower than their successors. The fourteenth-century Hall was eleven bays long and the Chapel seven. There is evidence that the Hall was originally intended to be smaller, but that an existing narrower building between it and the Kitchen Gate was demolished to first-floor level (its narrower undercroft still survives as the Steward's Room) and an additional five bays added to the length of the Hall. This suggests that there was an increase in the scale of the court ceremonial while Edward III's construction programme was rolling forward, and that the Hall was made grander as a result. With its lower ceiling and eleven bays, the visual effect and proportions of Edward III's Hall must have been closer to Wyatville's than Hugh May's. The original

J.C. BUCKLER: watercolour of the Steward's Room in 1860. Situated under the east end of St George's Hall, this room retains its Edward III vault.

WENZEL HOLLAR: engraving of St George's Hall in the reign of Charles II with the St George's Day feast in progress, from Ashmole's *Order of the Garter* (1672). This shows Edward III's original hall with its traceried timber roof and two tiers of windows.

timber roof with decorative tracery in the spandrels is recorded in Hollar's seventeenth-century engravings, before it was destroyed as part of Hugh May's reconstruction and heightening.

The scale and originality of design of the fourteenth-century work at Windsor Castle is such that it is a happy occurrence that the names of the master masons who directed the work under William of Wykeham are known.

John de Sponlee was the chief mason at Windsor Castle until 1361, when he retired because of age and failing health. He supervised the works in the Lower Ward and from 1351 was employed on the Upper Ward, where work proceeded clockwise, beginning with the Norman Gateway and concluding with the Devil's Tower, where work was still in progress at the time of Edward III's death in 1377. He was assisted in the Upper Ward by another mason, William of Wynford, who is recorded in 1360 as warden of the masons' work and in 1362 took over from Sponlee as principal mason. It seems highly likely that he was the chief influence on the design. He was subsequently the mason at William of Wykeham's two foundations, New College, Oxford (1380-86), and Winchester College (from 1387 onwards), both of which were very similar in design to the Hall-Chapel range at Windsor, suggesting that they were all designed by the same hand.

The work at Windsor was not completed by the time of Edward III's death, and continued for another six years into the reign of his grandson and successor Richard II. It remained, however, very much Edward's own achievement and it was his grandiose reconstruction which gave the Castle the pre-eminence among English royal residences which it has retained ever since.

Windsor is the only one of the medieval palaces to have been, more or less, continuously inhabited from the Middle Ages down to the present day. This is partly the result of the Castle's special association with the Order of the Garter, one of the oldest orders of Christian chivalry and probably the most influential.

On St George's Day, 1344, Edward III had held at Windsor a great tournament, the ritualized form of mock battle which had developed out of knightly training-in-arms into a splendid spectacle. He sent out his heralds to make known this event to France, Scotland, Burgundy, Flanders, Brabant, Germany and Lombardy. After it the King made a statement to the assembled knights that he was going to found a Round Table like that which King Arthur had established at Camelot. Nothing came of this romantic proposal immediately, but it was the overture to the chivalric order that the King established after his victorious return from France at the end of 1347. In August the following year he established by letters patent an order, called the Order of the Garter, of twenty-six Knights Companion, including himself. Many of them had been on the French campaign, and had taken part in the battle of Crécy. Their patron saint, as of England itself, was St George, a supposed officer of the Roman army, and their motto *'Honi soit qui mal y pense'* ('Shame on him who thinks this evil').

It is not known why the garter was chosen as the emblem of the new Order. Many legends attach to it, but the most plausible theory is that it was a badge which the English knights had adopted during the French campaign. The livery colours of the new Knights, deep blue and gold, were the colours of the French royal arms.

The original Knights were all young warriors, the military companions of the King and his son the Black Prince. Over subsequent centuries, however, the character of the Knights changed, and they came to be drawn from the ranks of leading nobles and statesmen, as well as foreign monarchs who were flattered to be asked to join; and the ceremonies of the Order increased in splendour, with glorious music, processions of heralds and a great feast taking place every year on St George's Day in April, when the whole court moved to Windsor. The court still is 'in residence' at Windsor in April each year, but the annual Garter celebration now takes place in June.

Just as the ceremonies of the Order were elaborated in the later medieval period, so was their architectural setting. Though the

THE BADGE OF THE ORDER OF THE GARTER. St George and the dragon are encircled by the Garter and the motto – *Honi soit qui mal y pense* (Shame on him who thinks this evil).

domestic quarters at Windsor remained largely as created by Edward III until the seventeenth century, the religious buildings in the Lower Ward continued to be altered and enlarged. In particular, in the fifteenth century Edward IV built a new and larger church, the present St George's Chapel. The work at St George's also included the semi-circular layout of brick and timber-framed

ST GEORGE'S CHAPEL. One of the great masterpieces of English Perpendicular Gothic, it was begun by Edward IV in 1475 and completed by Henry VII. It is the spiritual home of the Order of the Garter, founded by Edward III in 1348.

THE CLOISTERS, ST GEORGE'S CHAPEL. Built in the reign of Edward III for his new College of St George, they have fine Perpendicular tracery. The surrounding medieval buildings contain the houses of the Dean and Canons, a library and other subsidiary buildings, making a miniature cathedral close.

THE HORSESHOE CLOISTER IN THE LOWER WARD, WITH THE CURFEW TOWER BEHIND. The picturesque layout at the west end of St George's Chapel was originally built by Edward IV but was restored by Sir George Gilbert Scott for Queen Victoria. It contained the houses for the Vicars-choral. St George's Chapel is a collegiate foundation with Dean, Canons, and Choir of boys and men to sing the services.

houses for the Vicars-choral now known as the Horseshoe Cloisters. Begun in about 1475 under the direction of Richard Beauchamp, Bishop of Salisbury and Chancellor of the Order, St George's Chapel is the principal surviving architectural glory of medieval Windsor and one of the supreme achievements of English Perpendicular Gothic.

THE QUIRE OF ST GEORGE'S CHAPEL. The fifteenth-century choir stalls are surmounted by the crests and banners of the members of the Order of the Garter.

Only the choir, roofed in timber, was completed, under the direction of the mason Henry Janyns, by Edward IV's death in 1483. It was left to Henry VII (Edward's son-in-law) to complete the nave and to add the continuous ribbed stone vault which contributes so much to the magnificence and unity of the interior. A central tower was intended, but never completed. Henry VII also rebuilt Henry III's old Chapel to the east of St George's Chapel with the intention that it should serve as his burial place, but then changed his mind and built the Henry VII Chapel at Westminster Abbey instead.

From the start, St George's Chapel was richly furnished. The carved oak choir stalls with tall fretted canopies were made in 1478-85 by William Berkeley and the brass stall plates enamelled with the arms of the Knights of the Garter on the backs of the stalls, were transferred from the previous chapel, beginning a unique sequence of over seven hundred plates from the fourteenth down to the twentieth centuries.

ST GEORGE'S CHAPEL: detail of the Garter stall plates on the backs of the stalls, with the arms of the successive Knights of the Garter. This unique assemblage of heraldic art contains examples from the fourteenth century to the present day.

ST GEORGE'S CHAPEL: detail of the fifteenth-century choir stalls with the sovereign's stall on the south side of the entrance to the quire from the nave. The woodwork was brilliantly restored and extended in the true medieval spirit for George III by Henry Emlyn.

PAUL SANDBY: watercolour of the King Henry VIII Gate, which forms the principal entrance to the Lower Ward.

THE HENRY VIII GATE LOOKING THROUGH TO ST GEORGE'S CHAPEL, with soldiers marching back to barracks after Changing the Guard. The guard at Windsor is frequently formed of a battalion of one of the Household Regiments.

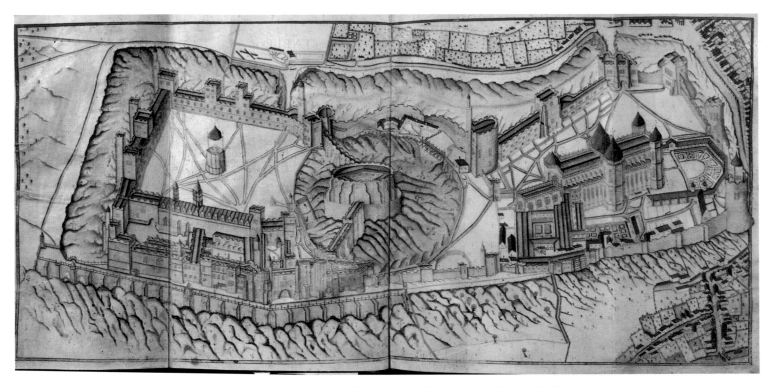

JOHN NORDEN: detail from the Survey map of Windsor made for James I in 1607. This depicts the Castle in the final form which it evolved in the Middle Ages. St George's Chapel, cloisters and the Dean and Canons' lodgings are on the right, and the royal palace round three courtyards on the left.

Apart from completing St George's Chapel, the Tudors laid a comparatively light hand on Windsor. Henry VII added a narrow range west of the State Apartments. Henry VIII built a new gateway (which bears his name) to the Lower Ward. Queen Mary built the lodgings for the Military Knights in the Lower Ward; Queen Elizabeth I added a Long Gallery to the west of the State Apartments (converted to the Royal Library in the nineteenth

JORIS HOEFNAGEL: pen-and-ink drawing of the Castle from the north in the reign of Elizabeth I.

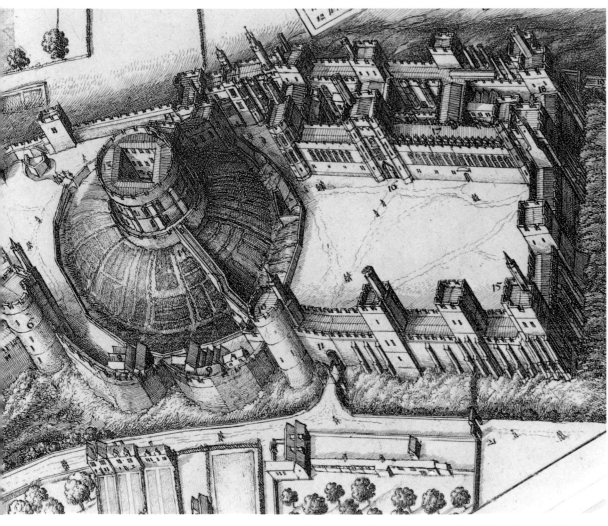

WENZEL HOLLAR: DETAIL OF A
BIRD'S-EYE VIEW OF WINDSOR
CASTLE, 1672, showing the Round
Tower and Upper Ward. Edward III's
palace on the north side is the basis of
the present State Apartments. It had
many unusual features, including the
balanced façade to the Quadrangle
with two entrance towers with turrets
and battlements. These were the
earliest examples in English architecture of the ornamental rather than
practical use of castle details.

century) and a terrace along the north side of the Upper Ward.

In the sixteenth and early seventeenth centuries, however, Windsor survived largely as a medieval building, and it was only the shock wave of the Civil War, the execution of Charles I and the Commonwealth, followed by the Restoration of the monarchy, that provoked a further substantial reconstruction of the Upper Ward.

CHAPTER TWO

CHARLES II

Baroque Reconstruction

The English Civil War in the middle of the seventeenth century marked a watershed in the history of Windsor, as of all the royal palaces, many of which were demolished during Oliver Cromwell's Protectorate and the Commonwealth. The Castle was seized by the Parliamentarians, who sacked St George's Chapel, melting down its plate and destroying its rich ornaments. The royal apartments in the Upper Ward were also sacked and used as a prison for captured Royalists. The Great Park was divided up into separate properties and sold off to supporters of the Commmonwealth, some of whom built houses there. The last sombre scene of Charles I's life took place at Windsor when he was quietly buried in St George's Chapel during a snow storm, following his execution at Whitehall in 1649.

At the Restoration of the monarchy in 1660 Charles II was determined to reinstate the old glories of the Crown. During the interval of the Commonwealth, only Whitehall and Hampton Court Palaces had been occupied by Cromwell, as Lord Protector, and the other royal residences when not totally demolished had been neglected and allowed to fall into disrepair.

One of Charles II's first acts was to commission splendid baroque crown jewels and rich chapel plate to replace the treasures melted down under the Commonwealth. The existing lavish silver-gilt altar plate of St George's Chapel was presented by Charles II in 1660-61.

He set about reconstituting the English royal residences on the strength of a revenue grant of £1,200,000 a year from Parliament. Unlike the modern civil list, this income was not a set sum. It consisted of the grant of specific revenues, chiefly the Customs and Excise, which it was hoped would bring in the promised amount of

WILLIAM DOBSON: *CHARLES II WHEN PRINCE OF WALES*, painted in 1644 when the Prince was fourteen and the outcome of the Civil War between the supporters of the King and Parliament still undecided.

REMBRANDT VAN RIJN: *AN OLD WOMAN*: 'The Artist's Mother', *c.* 1629. This was presented to Charles I and was the first Rembrandt in any English collection. One of the great treasures of the Royal Collection, it hangs in the King's Dressing Room.

money. But in fact it varied from year to year and fell substantially short of the desired sum. This left the King less well-off than intended and caused a royal financial crisis in 1672, which in turn curtailed many of the King's more ambitious palace-building projects.

Charles II also set out to recover as much as possible of the dispersed contents of the royal palaces. In June 1660 the diarist John Evelyn recorded that plate, hangings, pictures and so forth were daily being brought in. Seventeen cartloads of stuff were recovered from Cromwell's widow alone.

The great picture collection which had been formed by Charles I and hung mainly at Whitehall Palace was, however, mostly lost beyond recall, as many of the paintings had been sold on the Continent and acquired by the royal collections in Vienna, Paris and Madrid. Nevertheless Charles II was able to reassemble some of his father's treasures, notably the incomparable series of pictures by Sir Anthony van Dyck which now hang at Windsor. He was given many presents on his return to the throne, including a collection of

SIR ANTHONY VAN DYCK: *QUEEN HENRIETTA MARIA*, *c.* 1632. Charles I's magnificent collection of paintings was dispersed by order of Parliament during the Commonwealth. After the Restoration in 1660 Charles II reassembled all he could, including the incomparable series of Van Dyck portraits of the Stuart court which since the reign of Queen Victoria have been concentrated in the Queen's Ballroom at Windsor.

SIR ANTHONY VAN DYCK: *CHARLES I IN THREE POSITIONS*, *c.* 1635–6. This famous image of the King was painted to send to Bernini in Rome as a guide for carving a bust of the King (which was itself burnt in the fire at Whitehall).

SIR ANTHONY VAN DYCK: *THE FIVE ELDEST CHILDREN OF CHARLES I*, 1637. (*Left to right*): Princess Mary, Prince James, Prince Charles who rests his hand on the mastiff's head; Princess Elizabeth supports the infant Princess Anne.

LEONARD KNYFF: *WINDSOR CASTLE FROM THE NORTH, c. 1672.* Knyff was a Dutch artist who came to England, where he specialized in topographical views. The gigantic North Terrace was built by Elizabeth I and enlarged by Charles II.

pictures from the States-General of Holland and a magnificent set of silver furniture by the Corporation of the City of London.

Windsor was of special significance to Charles II and the Stuart dynasty. It was the only palace which could be effectively garrisoned – a not unimportant consideration after the recent upheavals. It housed St George's Chapel and St George's Hall, the headquarters of the Order of the Garter, England's prime order of chivalry, which was of special interest in the late seventeenth century, as is demonstrated by Elias Ashmole's history of the Order published in 1672 and Sir Peter Lely's well-known drawings of the Garter procession. Windsor was also the burial place of the King's martyred father, Charles I, and the King intended to erect a suitable mausoleum to his memory, though nothing came of this.

Charles II revived the ceremonies of the Order of the Garter immediately after the Restoration with an annual religious service for the Knights in St George's Chapel followed by a feast in St George's Hall. The dinner consisted of two courses and a dessert, served to the King by Gentlemen Pensioners, accompanied by the officers of the household, and to the Knights by the Yeomen of the Guard (founded by Henry VII), while musicians played in the gallery. Charles II sat on his own on the dais under a canopy of state while the Knights sat at a long table down the side of the Hall facing the windows. At the 1667 Garter feast, the courses comprised twenty-nine dishes each, including roasted pigs, wild boar pie and haggis puddings, followed by pheasants, lobsters and oysters. There was an interval between the courses, during which toasts were drunk and heralds processed down the centre of the Hall.

The provision of a suitable architectural setting for the ceremonies was a major impetus for the remodelling of the Upper Ward to create an up-to-date baroque palace within the castellated exterior. The reconstruction of Windsor was Charles II's major palace-building project and cost over £130,000. He chose as his architect not Sir Christopher Wren, the leading contemporary architect and Surveyor of the Office of Works, who was fully employed at the time rebuilding St Paul's Cathedral and the City churches following the Great Fire of London, but a less well-known contemporary architect, Hugh May.

Hugh May was the seventh son of a Sussex gentleman and had worked in the household of the Duke of Buckingham before the Civil War. During the Commonwealth he had joined the Stuart court in exile, and travelled extensively in Holland and France. At the Restoration he had been rewarded for his loyalty and services by being appointed Paymaster of Works, responsible for the financial side of the general overhaul of the derelict royal palaces. In 1668 he was promoted to the comptrollership of the Office of Works, under Wren. In November 1673 he was appointed to supervise the reconstruction of Windsor Castle.

May owed his promotion, as he told the diarist Samuel Pepys, to the kindness of the King. Though overshadowed by Wren, May was himself a distinguished architect who put to good use the experience he had gained while travelling on the Continent during the Commonwealth. He was responsible for introducing to England a mature baroque style of interior decoration which was a synthesis of the most recent architecture he had seen in Holland and France. In his interiors he combined the decorative arts, painting and carving to form one organized and unified architectural whole, gathering together at Windsor a team of artists and craftsmen to execute his ideas.

PAUL SANDBY: watercolour of the Castle from the Long Walk in the reign of George III. The Long Walk, an avenue over 2 miles (5 km) long was planted by Charles II to connect the Castle with the Great Park to the south.

He made extensive use of the talents of the Italian-born artist Antonio Verrio, who came to England in 1672, via France. He was brought over from Paris by the Duke of Montagu, Charles II's ambassador to Louis XIV, specially to execute the proposed painted decorations at Windsor, including mythologies, the history of the Order of the Garter and *trompe-l'oeil* ornament. They were his first significant work in England. He was later employed at Chatsworth in Derbyshire, Burghley in Northamptonshire and other country houses. The carver Grinling Gibbons also owed his first important commission in England to May. He played a key role in the decoration of the new baroque interior at Windsor Castle, embellishing the rooms with astonishing still-life carvings of fruit, flowers, birds or fish. They were his first public work and led to his being appointed Master Carver in Wood to the Crown, a post he held till the reign of George I. His predecessor in this post, Henry Phillips, also worked with Gibbons on the Windsor carvings.

The reconstruction of the Upper Ward of the Castle was carried out in two phases. The first phase – the provision of new State Apartments for the King and Queen – was executed in 1675-8. The second phase – the remodelling and redecoration of the Royal Chapel and St George's Hall – was begun in 1678. The structural work at Windsor was completed by 1680 and the interior decoration by 1684.

The result was both ingenious and magnificent, and made the Upper Ward into one of the most interesting baroque palaces in Europe. May's external work had a stripped-down, austere appearance, with round-arched windows surrounded by simple concave Portland stone architraves, and a blocky massiveness to the parts which harmonized well with the character of the medieval fortress. The east front was more or less symmetrical, with four towers and a central two-branched staircase leading to the *piano nobile*. Much of the north side was taken up by a large, plain new block known as the Star Building. This square block took its name from the large Garter star (12 ft (3.6 m) in diameter) on its façade. The Garter star had been added by Charles I to the Garter regalia for everyday wear by the Knights rather than the more cumbersome collar worn on ceremonial occasions. The van Dyck portraits of the King show the star prominently displayed.

THE KING'S DINING ROOM: detail of the wood carvings by Grinling Gibbons, which take the form of three-dimensional still lifes incorporating fruit, flowers and pea pods.

The interior was in rich contrast and formed the first and grandest sequence of baroque state apartments in England. Like the state rooms at Hampton Court, the Windsor rooms represent in their most extended form a royal state enfilade. Their plan is the product of centuries of evolution from the thirteenth to the seventeenth centuries.

In order to understand them, it is necessary to know something of the way in which these rooms developed and were originally intended to be used. The basic function of the Court was to regulate and formalize contact between the sovereign and his more important subjects. Access to the King or Queen was the objective of every courtier, and the essential problem in planning a royal palace was to arrange a succession of rooms which would ensure an orderly progression for those with the privilege of access – the entrée – and would also provide the monarch with private rooms where he could retire.

In early times the only essential rooms in a palace were the Hall and Chamber, but in the Middle Ages a more elaborate sequence of rooms had developed, so that it was usual for both the King and the Queen each to have their own separate apartments and chapels. This duality of twin state apartments is one of the distinctive features of Windsor Castle from the thirteenth century until the end of the eighteenth century. They only ceased to be used in the time of George IV, who was estranged from his wife and did not occupy the old State Apartments but created new and more luxurious royal apartments for himself in the east and south ranges of the Upper Ward.

The number of rooms in each apartment multiplied as their functions became more specialized and more complex, a process which, like many of the features of the seventeenth- and eighteenth-century household, had begun under Henry VIII. He was determined to secure more privacy and to devise a means of keeping away from courtiers who were trying to catch his eye or find him off guard in order to ask for some inconvenient favour or other. Henry VIII even forbade the courtiers to follow him when he was hunting. To avoid being besieged by the court he was forced to regulate the distance between himself and his courtiers by increasing the number of rooms and guarding their access more strictly. Where once there had just been the Chamber, there was now the Guard Chamber, the Presence Chamber, the Privy Chamber and the Bed Chamber. Each of these rooms had a specific function. The Guard Chamber contained the Yeomen of the Guard; royal audiences were given in the Presence Chamber; the Privy Chamber was a private room for the King to retire to, adjoining his Bed Chamber. The royal household ordinances promulgated by Henry VIII at Eltham Palace in 1526 clearly defined access to these various rooms. 'Lords, knights, gentlemen, officers of the king's house and other honest personages' were allowed entrance to the Presence Chamber, but entrance to the Privy Chamber was more carefully restricted. 'Noe person, of what estate, degree or condicion soever he be, from henceforth presume, attempt or be in any wise suffered or admitted to come or repair into the king's privy chamber' except the servants on duty and persons invited by the King himself. As for the Bed Chamber, no one was allowed to enter except the King's personal servants.

The King himself emerged from his private rooms only for some specific purpose, such as going to the Chapel or for public ceremony or entertainment. He was careful to make these daily public ceremonies as magnificent as possible, and this court pageantry was maintained and elaborated by his Tudor and Stuart successors to enhance the majesty of their position. The Stuarts, in particular, lost no opportunity to emphasize that they ruled by Divine Right.

As time passed, and the monarch retreated further, so the courtiers pressed beyond the outer rooms, leading to an ever longer enfilade. The strict privacy of the Privy Chamber, as proclaimed by Henry VIII, was given up in the seventeenth century. In the reign of Charles I, the right of entry to the Queen's Privy Chamber was granted to the nobility, and it is probable that the King's too was open to courtiers in general. At the Restoration the Lord Mayor of London, Sir Richard Leveson, reported that the 'Court is modelling itself as it was in the late King's time, that is, that persons are to come near the King's person as they are in quality.' Charles II confirmed in his Household Regulations that persons waiting for business could enter the King's Privy Chamber. Thus by the mid-seventeenth century the Privy Chamber was only slightly less public than the Presence Chamber. Its place as a private room between the public state apartment and the King's Bed Chamber was taken by the Withdrawing Room. Such a room was in existence as early as 1627 in the Queen's apartment at Whitehall and access to it was by personal invitation only, not by traditional right. By the late seventeenth century the Withdrawing Room had undergone the same process of diminishing privacy as the Privy Chamber, and it in turn became the main room of assembly. When the Grand Duke of Tuscany, for instance, visited Whitehall Palace in 1669, he was received by Charles II in the Withdrawing Room.

Just as the royal household developed and split into specific subdivisions in the sixteenth and seventeenth centuries, so the state apartment divided into rooms designed to serve different aspects of the royal persona: rooms for state, public rooms for society and the King's private rooms. One after the other the state rooms lost their original functions and became merely ante-rooms to the Drawing Room, which thus became the principal place for court assemblies. There the King most often met court society or received important foreigners.

Important visitors to the royal palaces approached by way of a courtyard and a grand staircase, and at the head of the stairs entered the Guard Chamber and then passed through the Presence and Privy Chambers into the Drawing Room, beyond which were the King's or Queen's private apartments. Each room retained its appropriate attendants – Yeomen of the Guard in the Guard Chamber, Gentlemen Ushers in the Presence Chamber, Gentlemen of the King's Chamber in the Privy Chamber, and the Groom of the Stole in the Drawing Room and the private rooms beyond – Bed Chamber, Closet and so forth. Each of the principal reception rooms might still boast its canopy of state, marking the place where the King had once stood or sat, one, two or three hundred years before. Thus the history of the English court was encapsulated in the enfilade of the state apartment as it existed in the seventeenth and eighteenth centuries.

Access to the more distant rooms in the long state enfilade continued to be restricted according to rank. This was regulated once again by Charles II in his Household Ordinances after the Restoration. In January 1685 Sir Charles Lyttelton wrote:

> There is another thing which is now as much talked on: the new orders about the bedchamber ... Nobody except the Duke [of York], Lord Ormonde, and I think Halifax, the two Secretaries of England and the Secretaries of Scotland are to come into the bedchamber without leave first asked; nor are they to ask leave if the King be in the closet. None under the degree of nobleman or privy councillor may ask leave at all, unless he has business with the King.

By the early nineteenth century the modern arrangement had emerged, where a variable number of ante-rooms with no specific function (just a guard room in a newly-built palace such as Buckingham Palace but a series of fossilized state apartments in older palaces such as Windsor) led to the entrée room for grandees, peers or accredited ambassadors to wait in, and then the Throne Room itself where the monarch received. All these chambers made a clearer separation possible between the public and private lives of the monarch. George III and then Queen Victoria took the process to a logical conclusion by building independent private houses for quiet family life in addition to the state palaces used for the monarch's official business.

Throughout the seventeenth and eighteenth and into the nineteenth centuries the English court was the chief focus of the nation's social life and its perambulations determined the London season. In the winter – approximately from October or November to mid-May – the King was based at Whitehall Palace, or later at St James's Palace. In the summer he moved to one or other of the country palaces, Windsor Castle or Hampton Court. The exact dates of his moves were determined by the weather and, in time, by the meeting of Parliament.

Attendance at court was the essential qualification for being 'in' socially. This meant, above all, going to the royal drawing-rooms (the event taking its name from the place of assembly). They were held several evenings a week in the eighteenth century, though they became less regular later and were discontinued by Queen Victoria after the death of Prince Albert in 1861. Drawing-rooms were stiff,

formal and rather dull occasions on the whole, though it is recorded that one man was thrown out for being 'drunk and saucy' at St James's Palace in 1718. The King usually stood or sat at one end of the room and spoke to those who were nearest to him, the company forming a respectful semi-circle round him. The qualification for attendance was not as clearly defined as at some of the more hidebound Continental courts, and a certain amount of leeway was left for healthy social-climbing. The need to wear fashionable (i.e. expensive) clothes seems to have been the chief deterrent to the unworthy. Quality and style of dress therefore decided who got in on general court days, but the etiquette was stricter on court show days, such as the King's birthday and the anniversaries of his coronation and accession to the throne. There were also occasional court balls and morning levees (the latter for men only). Ministers (including foreign emissaries), great nobles and the major gentry

SIR PETER PAUL RUBENS, *PORTRAIT OF THE ARTIST*, 1622. Rubens, like Van Dyck, worked in London for the English Crown. This picture formed part of Charles I's collection.

formed the core of those who usually attended court.

An important development in the seventeenth century was a substantial decrease in the size of the royal household under Charles II. This was caused mainly by rapidly rising costs and the resulting pressure for retrenchment. In the course of the century whole sub-offices were abolished – several medieval court offices, including the Esquire of the Body and many ancient sporting posts – and individual posts left unfilled. Statistics help to tell the story. In Charles I's reign there were 46 posts in the Hall; by 1714 only 5 survived. In the early seventeenth century there were 200 Yeomen of the Guard; in 1700 there were 100. Under Charles I there were 97 grooms in the stables; under George I there were only 72. In the course of the seventeenth century the household below stairs decreased from 300 to 160 people. Altogether the royal household was reduced from 1450 servants under Charles I to 950 under

JOHN RILEY: *BRIDGET HOLMES WITH APRON AND BROOM*, 1686. Mrs Riley, the 'necessary woman' was ninety-six years old when this portrait was painted in the reign of James II and had worked at the Castle since the reign of Charles I. She lived to be a hundred. The junior page is probably Tobias Rustat, later Yeoman of the Robes, who gave the statue of Charles II in the Quadrangle.

George I. This reduction meant that less accommodation was needed for permanent inhabitants, while at the same time more space was needed for public rooms as the governing class and the social élite (synonymous in the seventeenth century) increased in numbers.

These underlying changes in the structure, arrangement and purpose of the court were the practical background to the architectural reconstruction of Windsor Castle carried out for Charles II in the 1670s and 1680s. The Castle remained largely as he left it for over a hundred years.

As usual in England there were duplicated sets of State Apartments for the King and the Queen. They were approached through a ground-floor vestibule with Ionic columns (two of the capitals survive in the China Museum) and niches in the walls containing antique busts. The Queen's Great Staircase, on axis with the entrance from the Upper Ward, was a remarkable ensemble with dramatic lighting, partly through a glazed cupola in the domed ceiling and partly through an oval opening in the back wall revealing further spaces beyond. This gave an added dimension to the illusionistic paintings by Antonio Verrio. The King's Grand Staircase at the east end of the Horn Court was approached through open arcades along the sides. The standard sequences of state rooms were arranged on the *piano nobile* round the Brick and Horn Courts.

The decoration in all these rooms was of striking novelty and set a fashion which was copied in most of the state apartments of private houses in late seventeenth century England, with the result that Burghley, Northamptonshire, or Chatsworth, Derbyshire, now give a better idea of the lost splendours of Windsor than the present appearance of the state rooms there. The walls were wainscotted, and festooned with amazing virtuoso carvings by Henry Phillips and Grinling Gibbons of fruit, flowers, fish and game, rather like Dutch still-life paintings transformed into three dimensions. The gilding was by René Cousin, a Frenchman. The source of inspiration for the work in general was the France of Louis XIV, but the use of wood rather than coloured marbles gave Windsor a different character from the contemporary interiors at Versailles. Verrio's ceiling paintings were an important feature. By 1678 he had completed thirteen of them, all with fulsomely propagandist subjects – the Restoration of the monarchy, the re-establishment of the Church of England, Charles II triumphing over factions, and a general mingling of royal glory and classical mythology.

Altogether the new State Apartments at Windsor Castle comprised fifteen rooms. Both the King's and Queen's Apartments had individual Staircases and Guard Chambers and comprised a Presence Chamber, Audience Chamber, Drawing Room, Bed Chamber and Closet. In addition, the King had another room which was his private Bedroom, and a Dining Room, while the Queen had a Ballroom or Gallery as an additional entertaining room between her Audience Chamber and Drawing Room. The sumptuous decoration of these rooms, orchestrated by Hugh May, represented the

CHARLES WILD: watercolour of the Queen's Ballroom in the reign of George III. Verrio's painted ceiling and the carved oak wainscot on the walls were standard throughout the Charles II state rooms. Most of them were remodelled for George IV and William IV, only the cornices by Grinling Gibbons generally surviving. The silver furniture reflected an extravagant royal fashion started by Louis XIV at Versailles.

'golden glow of Restoration Triumphalism'. The Queen's Great Staircase, at the west end of the Horn Court, was painted by Verrio with *trompe-l'oeil* architecture, a figure of Time, and Ovidean scenes of the transformation of Phaeton's sisters into trees and of Cygnus into a swan. These feigned decorations were reinforced by real sculptures including bronzes of a Roman vestal and the Spinario and a black marble Venus.

The Queen's Guard Chamber had decorative trophies and wheel arrangements of arms and armour on the walls; and the illusionistic ceiling was painted by Verrio with the tribute of the four continents being presented to Britannia (a portrait of Catherine of Braganza,

Charles II's consort) in a central oval panel framed by a snake biting its tail.

The Queen's Presence Chamber was panelled in oak with a carved cornice of crisp acanthus leaves, and festoons of carved fruit and flowers by Grinling Gibbons and Henry Phillips, framing a portrait over the marble bolection moulded fireplace. This wall treatment was standard throughout all the Hugh May State Apartments. The ceiling, painted by Verrio, again showed Queen Catherine of Braganza, seated under a canopy held by zephyrs

while figures of Envy and Sedition retreat before the outstretched sword of Justice. It still survives, as does that in the Queen's Audience Chamber, which depicts Catherine of Braganza being drawn across the skies in a chariot by swans towards a temple of virtue; while the cove of the ceiling is treated as a *trompe-l'oeil* marble balustrade, as in Le Brun's contemporary painted ceilings at Versailles. The flying figures, sky and clouds of the central field, however, owe more to the work of Pietro da Cortona and other Italian seicento artists than to Versailles.

The Queen's Gallery or Ballroom had a pair of marble bolection chimneypieces and lavishly carved overmantels by Grinling Gibbons,

THE QUEEN'S AUDIENCE CHAMBER: ceiling painted by Antonio Verrio, showing Catherine of Braganza (wife of Charles II) being drawn in a chariot of swans towards a temple of virtue, and the cove treated as a balustrade. The general form is inspired by Le Brun's work for Louis XIV at Versailles.

seducing Danae and Leda respectively. These painted ceilings were much admired at the time. The diarist John Evelyn wrote: 'Verrio's invention is admirable; his figures move.'

All these rooms were uniformly treated as a suite with marble bolection chimneypieces, oak wainscot on the walls, carved festooned overmantels and carved acanthus friezes. The latter generally survived the later remodellings. So also did much of the decorative ensemble in the King's Dining Room, situated between the King's Apartment and the Queen's Drawing Room. Its ceiling (surviving) formed a pendant to that in the latter and shows a banquet of the gods, and the cove is painted with enticing still lifes of fish and fowl, including a bright red lobster. The carved festoons by Gibbons and Phillips framing the overmantel were likewise composed of brilliantly executed fruit, fish, game and shellfish.

Today, the Dining Room alone gives some impression of the appearance of Hugh May's King's Apartment, just as the Queen's Presence and Audience Chambers represent the character of Catherine of Braganza's rooms.

The climax of Hugh May's reconstruction of Windsor was the redecoration in 1680-84 of St George's Hall and the King's Chapel within the shell of Edward III's building and substantial structural changes: the Chapel was extended at the expense of the Hall to create two rooms of more equal dimensions. At the same time the range was heightened by a half storey with an additional line of upper windows, treated in the Hall as circles with painted garters for their frames – a charmingly appropriate idea.

The Hall walls were painted by Verrio with feigned columns and grand historical setpieces showing the Black Prince's triumphal reception by Edward III; and the ceiling with Charles II in Garter robes enthroned in glory. The floor was paved with black and white marble, and at one end, on a dais, was a glorious baroque throne, richly gilded and supported by carved figures of slaves, the work of Louis van Opstal and John van der Stein. The overall scheme was symbolic of would-be absolutism as well as being a splendid setting for the Garter ceremonies. The throne had a short life, being removed by William III after the Glorious Revolution in 1688 and replaced by a portrait of himself.

The adjoining Chapel was even more spectacular. Its decoration formed a remarkable unity. The walls and ceilings were covered with an integrated scheme of paintings by Verrio, depicting Christ's miracles behind a feigned marble colonnade along the walls and

THE KING'S DINING ROOM: detail of Antonio Verrio's painted ceiling. The cove has realistic still lifes of fish, fowl, fruit and other edible delights.

CHARLES WILD: watercolour of St George's Hall as remodelled for Charles II to the design of Hugh May. The destruction of this room in 1829 is one of the great losses of English architecture as it was a baroque masterpiece. Verrio's paintings depicted the history of Edward III and the Black Prince and the Order of the Garter. A particularly attractive feature was the circular windows framed by painted Garters. The central oval ceiling panel showed Charles II in glory.

culminating in a huge painting of the Ascension on the ceiling. Behind the altar was a small apse with a painting of the Last Supper framed by columns, inspired by Bernini's *baldacchino* in St Peter's, Rome, with gilded capitals and vast swags of flowers. Some of this ensemble was *trompe-l'oeil* painting and some of it carved and gilded wood. The semi-dome over the altar was open to reveal the gilded pipes of a concealed organ behind, a feature much admired by Evelyn. Round the lower parts of the walls were magnificent carved wooden stalls, their backs embellished with sprays of palm and laurel by Grinling Gibbons. The royal tribune was decorated by Gibbons with 'six Vasses with thistles Roses and two Boyes Laurel and Palmes and other Ornaments in the Front and upon the Topp of

the King's seate with Drapery, Fruit, Flowers, Crootesses, Starres, Roses'.

These Windsor rooms 'set a new decorative ideal in England, but the scale and splendour of May's hall and chapel were never achieved again'. The only comparable room is the Painted Hall at the Royal Naval College, Greenwich, which, though by James Thornhill rather than Verrio, still gives some idea of the vanished baroque splendours of Windsor. Charles II's Hall and Chapel were, unfortunately, destroyed in 1829 to make way for Wyatville's new St George's Hall, though some of Grinling Gibbons's virtuoso wood carvings were reused to decorate the Waterloo Chamber and other rooms in the Castle. Nearly the complete enfilade of the Queen's

CHARLES WILD: *THE KING'S CHAPEL*. This, like Charles II's St George's Hall, was destroyed to make way for Wyatville's larger hall in 1829, though some of Grinling Gibbon's carvings of palm fronds were reused in the Waterloo Chamber. Verrio's paintings included *The Last Supper* behind the altar. The gilded organ pipes visible above were real, and the whole design formed a brilliant baroque fusion of three-dimensional and painted *trompe-l'oeil* architecture.

state rooms (apart from the Bed Chamber which is now part of the Royal Library) and half of the King's rooms still survive, however, as planned by Charles II, though most of them have lost their Verrio ceilings.

Charles II's remodelling of Windsor Castle extended to the grounds and parks. The Upper Ward was formalized to make a regular Quadrangle with, in the centre, a bronze equestrian statue of Charles II. This was only the second equestrian bronze statue to be executed in England and was deliberately conceived as a pendant to the other: Hubert Le Sueur's masterly sculpture of Charles I at

QUEEN'S BALLROOM: SILVER TABLE BY ANDREW MOORE, *c. 1695*, part of a set of silver furniture presented to William III from the City of London. This and the similar set, comprising table, mirror and pair of candle stands, presented to Charles II are rare survivals of a short-lived royal taste. All Louis XIV's furniture at Versailles, which inspired the fashion, had to be melted down to pay for his European wars.

Whitehall which, miraculously, had survived the Commonwealth because the craftsman ordered to melt it down had hidden it instead. The equestrian Charles II at Windsor was cast in 1679 by a German sculptor, Josias Ibach, from Bremen. The plinth was carved in marble by Grinling Gibbons with characteristic naturalistic festoons and garlands.

On the north side of the Upper Ward, Charles II widened the central part of Elizabeth I's terrace, giving it a more baroque form as the foreground to Hugh May's Star Building containing the King's Apartments.

Charles II's major formal gesture was reserved for the south side of the Castle where he bought back and reconstituted the Great Park. An avenue of four rows of elms, the Long Walk, two and a half miles (4.25 km) long, was planted in 1683-5, leading to the Great Park. Though replanted in 1945 after the old trees succumbed to elm disease, this still gives the best idea of the scale and bravura of Charles II's remodelling of Windsor as his major country palace.

Further improvements were made to the gardens at Windsor by William III and Queen Anne. Various schemes for a vast ornamental parterre were conceived for the area below the north terrace stretching as far as the river. The Maestricht Garden was begun here by William III, but never completed. In 1698 the architect Nicholas Hawksmoor produced a scheme for remodelling the façade of the south range of the Upper Ward in a monumental classical manner, but this remained on paper. William III's reconstruction of Hampton Court in the 1690s gave it precedence as the sovereign's favourite summer palace. Queen Anne continued to use the Castle as an occasional residence, but in the first half of the eighteenth century the Hanoverian kings, George I and George II, used Hampton Court as their English summer palace and rarely visited the Castle. Windsor, however, after this brief slumber, came back into its own in the reign of George III, who disliked Hampton Court, which had unhappy memories for him, and enthusiastically adopted Windsor instead. All the subsequent monarchs of the United Kingdom have resided there.

BRONZE EQUESTRIAN STATUE OF CHARLES II IN THE QUADRANGLE OF THE UPPER WARD. Cast in 1679 by the German Josias Ibach, this was only the second equestrian statue of an English monarch, being inspired by LeSueur's Charles I at Whitehall. The carved panels in the plinth are by Grinling Gibbons, the leading member of the team of brilliant craftsmen employed by Charles II to restore the Castle after the Civil War and Commonwealth.

CHAPTER THREE

GEORGE III

Return to Windsor

George III came to the throne in 1760 as a young man of twenty-two. The gossip and socialite Horace Walpole wrote in January 1761: 'The King and Lord Bute [his tutor and first Prime Minister] have both of them a great propensity to the arts. Building, I am told, is the King's favourite study.' He had been taught architecture as part of his education by William Chambers, whom he now appointed Surveyor General.

The young King immediately put into effect some of his ideas by commissioning Chambers to remodel Buckingham House in London as a new royal residence, and to produce designs for an entirely new country palace at Richmond which in the event were not to be executed. He never wanted to see Hampton Court again: it reverberated, still, in his mind with the quarrels between his father, Frederick, Prince of Wales, and his grandfather George II. He began to think of a *pied-à-terre* at Windsor as he was attracted to the place, particularly by the park. In the event it was Windsor, rather than Richmond or Kew, which the King adopted as his principal country house.

During the reigns of George I and George II, much of the Upper Ward had been parcelled out as grace-and-favour apartments among private residents, many of them widows. Mrs Kennedy lived in Henry II's Tower. Mrs Margaret Trevor had an apartment in the Quadrangle. Mrs Egerton had the north-east tower and Mrs Walsingham a suite of rooms at the south side to the east of Edward III's tower.

The King therefore tried to persuade his brother, Henry Frederick, Duke of Cumberland, to give up the Rangership of Windsor Great Park in which office he had succeeded their uncle,

THOMAS GAINSBOROUGH: *KING GEORGE III, 1781.* The King wears the Garter Star and Riband, and the Windsor uniform coat of dark blue with gold facings and red collar and cuffs which he designed for formal wear at the Castle.

PAUL SANDBY: *CUMBERLAND LODGE IN THE GREAT PARK.* This was the home of successive Dukes of Cumberland, uncle and nephew, who were Rangers of Windsor Great Park and responsible for many landscape improvements, including the creation of Virginia Water, an artificial lake.

William Augustus, Duke of Cumberland, in 1765. This would have freed the Ranger's house in the Park, Cumberland Lodge, but despite being offered £6,000 a year the Duke declined. In June 1776 George III decided to take over the small brick house to the south of the Castle which had occasionally been occupied by Queen Anne as a lodge for stag-hunting, and of which she was very fond. It had latterly been occupied by the Lord Steward, but had recently become empty. George III wrote to Lord North (who had succeeded Bute as Prime Minister): 'the Queen expressed a strong wish that, as Queen Anne had lived there, I would give it to her; this will give us the means of some pleasant jaunts to that beautiful Park.'

The house became known as the Upper Lodge but more usually as the Queen's Lodge. It was too small for the royal family, and from 1778 Sir William Chambers supervised the commission to rebuild it on a larger scale at an eventual cost of over £40,000 but still as a private *pied-à-terre*. The result was a big plain house with round-headed windows intended to match May's in the Upper Ward. The result looked rather like a barracks. The King told a friend that he started with the idea of a lodge for himself and the Queen to sleep in occasionally when he came to Windsor to hunt or for picnics and excursions in the Park, and to avoid the inconvenience of returning to London or Kew in the evening. Had he been able to foresee that Windsor would become their 'chosen residence' he would have repaired the Castle from the start and resided there. He later told the architect James Wyatt that Sir William Chambers had advised him that the Castle could not be made comfortably habitable and advised him to build the Queen's Lodge instead.

The King and Queen lived informally at the Queen's Lodge, much in the public eye, and moving among the people of Windsor 'with the freedom of a small squire in a country village'. The Castle precincts and State Apartments were regularly open to the general public throughout the eighteenth century, and the Castle was much used as a playground by local schoolchildren. Charles Knight, the son of a Windsor bookseller, recorded in later life:

CLOCK with gilt bronze and blue-john case made by Matthew Boulton to the designs of Sir William Chambers and George III, 1770–71.

> *The deserted courts of the Upper Quadrangle often re-echoed on the moon-lit winter evenings with our whoo-whoop. The rooks and a few antique dowagers, who had each their domiciles in some lone turret of that spacious square, were the only personages who were disturbed by our revelry. In the magnificent playground of the Terrace, along we went along the narrow wall, and even the awful height of the north side could not abate the rash courage of follow my leader ... the park was a glory for cricket and kite-flying. The King would stand alone to see the boys at cricket. He was a quiet, good-humoured gentleman in a long blue coat; and many a time had he bidden us good morning when we were hunting for mushrooms in the early dew and he was returning from his dairy to his eight o'clock break fast. Everyone knew that most respectable and amiable of country squires, and His Majesty knew everyone.*

The precincts and terraces were accessible without formality, though the sentries had orders to prevent nuisances, keep out hawkers and control unruly children. In 1781 the Castle Governor issued the following instructions:

> *The sentries at the Round Tower, King's and Town Gates, are to keep every thing quiet about their respective posts. No beggars or disorderly persons are upon any account to be allowed to pass their posts and no coaches are to be allowed to stand in any of the Gate ways ... The sentries at the King's Gate and Governor's Door, are not to permit any servants or boys to gallop about the court. No higglers to be allowed to bring any meat, fish or greens to sell in the Court Yard of the palace, nor are any articles to be cried out for sale in any part of the palace. No beggars or disorderly person, women in red cloaks or pattens are to be allowed to walk upon the Terrace at any time.*

PAUL SANDBY: *THE LOWER WARD LOOKING WEST FROM THE BASE OF THE ROUND TOWER, c.* 1760. The lodgings of the Military Knights are on the left, St George's Chapel in the centre and the Winchester Tower on the right.

The State Apartments were open to the public on application to the Housekeeper. Regular guidebooks to the rooms were published. In 1749 Joseph Pote, a bookseller at Eton, was given a royal licence to publish the *History and Antiquities of Windsor Castle.* In 1755 he also published a 'lesser work on the same subject, and extracted from the above History, in French, and English, for the Use and Accomodation of Strangers, and other Persons who visit this Royal Castle'. It was called *Les Delices de Windsore*, and was the predecessor of the modern guidebooks to the Castle; it sold for 2s. Pote's guide included a plan 'Shewing Alphabetically at one View the several Appartments in the Royal Palace as shewn to ye Publicke'. The rooms available to be visited in the late eighteenth century were virtually identical to those open to the public in 1996 and chiefly comprised Charles II's King's and Queen's State Apartments.

The King loved playing the role of country squire – Farmer George at Windsor. On the death of Henry Frederick, Duke of Cumberland in 1790 he finally took over the direct management of Windsor Great Park. William Augustus, Duke of Cumberland – Ranger from 1746-65 – had carried out a series of large-scale landscaping projects in the Park with the advice of the artist Thomas Sandby and the architect Henry Flitcroft, planting trees, making new drives, erecting an obelisk and other decorative structures. The latter included the creation of Virginia Water, a large and picturesque lake at the southern end of the Park, with a cascade and grotto, a Chinese tea house, and two towers on the surrounding hilltops. Thomas Sandby continued to act as architect and Deputy Ranger for Henry Frederick, Duke of Cumberland, after 1765. But after the collapse of the Virginia Water pondhead in 1768 the southern area of the Park was neglected until in 1781 the King announced that it was to be restored. The enlarged lake, with a new cascade and grotto further to the east, was thus the responsibility of George III, but it was undertaken – at least initially – to the

JOSEPH MALLORD WILLIAM
TURNER: *WINDSOR CASTLE FROM
THE GREAT PARK*, 1793.

designs of Cumberland's architect, Sandby. George III also reclaimed large areas of the Park to the north and north-west for agriculture. He laid out two big farms with the advice of Nathaniel Kent, a leading agricultural theorist of the period, who set up the first specialist firm of land agents in London, and whose *Hints to Gentlemen of Landed Property*, published in 1775, was widely read by all ranks of landowners. Each of the two new farms was managed according to a different pattern of cultivation: the Norfolk Farm of

PAUL SANDBY: watercolour of the North Terrace with visitors, in the reign of George III. The Castle precincts and State Apartments were generally open to the public in the eighteenth century and a guidebook to the Castle was published by an Eton bookseller.

THOMAS GAINSBOROUGH: *QUEEN CHARLOTTE, 1781.* Gainsborough's sensitive portrait of the Queen is the best image of her. The dress is a *tour de force* of brushwork. Gainsborough and his nephew, Gainsborough Dupont, spent a whole night in their studio painting it.

Two years later the lease of the adjoining estate, Great Frogmore, was purchased for £8,000. The combined properties were entrusted to the Queen as her personal property to remodel and improve according to her own taste. She first devoted herself to the grounds, which were landscaped with the help of the Revd Mr Alderson, 'a man of great natural taste, but not of the world', and the ornamental lake formed according to the design of the Vice-Chamberlain of her household, Major William Price, brother of Uvedale Price, the Squire of Foxley in Herefordshire and apostle of the Picturesque. From 1793 the house at Great Frogmore was remodelled for her by the architect who came to succeed Sir William Chambers as the favourite of the royal family, James Wyatt. Following Chambers's death in 1796, the King promoted Wyatt to the post of Surveyor-General.

Wyatt probably came to the King's attention at the time of the opening of his first major building in London, the Pantheon in Oxford Street, in 1772, and may have been presented to the King by Richard Dalton, the royal librarian, whom Wyatt had met in Venice while on his Grand Tour in the 1760s.

Wyatt, as his first work for the Queen, designed with Princess Elizabeth some of the ornamental buildings scattered about as focal points in the new layout, including a rustic hermit's cottage and a Gothic ruin, which contained a room decorated with 'Tudor' paintings where the Queen sometimes had breakfast in summer. At first the Queen thought of replacing the house at Little Frogmore with a new Gothic 'cottage'. On 13 January 1792, she wrote to Prince Augustus:

> *Wyatt the Architect has made me the prittiest plan imaginable for a Gothic cottage, it consists of four rooms upon a Floor besides the Towers of which there are 4 which will make eight closets alotted for Books, Plants, China and one for the Flower pieces painted by Miss mosert [sic]. There will be a colonnade the whole length of the house which will make a sweet retirement in the summer all dressed out with Flowers.*

Wyatt prepared several different designs for Little Frogmore, and the following year the Queen wrote to the Earl of Ailesbury that he had 'made many pretty tantalizing proposals about my little paradise'. In the event the Gothic style was abandoned altogether and instead the house at Great Frogmore, which dated from the 1680s, was remodelled, stuccoed and enlarged in the classical style.

QUEEN CHARLOTTE'S SEDAN CHAIR, c. 1770.

Wyatt added an extra storey, flanking pavilions with segmental bowed centres, and pairs of characteristic tripartite windows using Doric columns as mullions. This order was continued to the same scale in the Doric colonnade the length of the west front (now glazed, but originally open), which tied the whole composition together and gave the enlarged house an overall architectural consistency and unity. Wyatt also partially remodelled the adjoining stables, an attractive eighteenth-century ensemble with two square towers carrying little domed caps and sporting a sundial and a clock.

CHARLES WILD: *FROGMORE, THE GREEN PAVILION.* Frogmore in the Home Park at Windsor was remodelled for Queen Charlotte as a trianon by James Wyatt.

The interior of Frogmore House was arranged to show the Queen's collections to advantage, and though much of Wyatt's elegant neo-classical decoration has disappeared, the appearance of the rooms as they were in Queen Charlotte's lifetime is recorded in Pyne's *Royal Residences*. In the south pavilion was 'Miss Moser's Room', with large flower paintings by Mary Moser for which she was paid £900. The upholstery in the room was painted to match with floral motifs on black, and Wyatt designed an unusual chimneypiece of white marble 'so pure it looks like alabaster', with rams' head consoles and *trompe-l'oeil* frieze carved with fringed drapery, an enchanting conceit. The central room in the south pavilion was the dining room, with apsed ends and a blue, red-and-white colour scheme; on the walls hung a series of Mecklenburg-Strelitz family portraits. Pyne described this exquisite but austere room as being 'fitted up in a style of elegant simplicity, in conformity with the notions of her Majesty'. The adjoining library has been dismantled but had cases grained to resemble satinwood, the walls painted brown to tone in with them. Along the top of the cases were black plaster busts of literary figures. Other rooms of special interest were the various Japan rooms fitted with red and black lacquer wall

CHARLES WILD: *QUEEN CHARLOTTE'S LIBRARY AT FROGMORE.* This handsome room was designed by James Wyatt. The bookcases were grained to represent satinwood, with bronzed busts round the top. The Queen kept her own collection at Frogmore and used to spend the day there with her daughters.

panels, some genuine and some imitation painted by Princess Elizabeth, George III's talented younger daughter. She spent much of her time at Frogmore with her mother pursuing their shared interests, painting and botanical collections; the Queen even had a printing press there. The Queen does not appear to have slept in the house but used merely to spend the day, going over from Windsor to pursue her own interests there.

The royal family was pleased with Wyatt's work at Frogmore and before long he was entrusted with the transformation of Windsor Castle itself. According to Joseph Farington, the Royal Academician and diarist:

Wyatt did not receive any [financial] compensation for the trouble and loss of time which he had suffered in the attendance of the Queen and Princess [Elizabeth] building Frogmore etc ... Indeed Wyatt told a person that the expenses and great loss of time in attending upon the royal Family had been the ruin of him.

George III was aware of this and it was by way of recompense that he appointed him Surveyor-General.

Despite the debilitating effect of these royal commissions on his architectural practice James Wyatt obviously derived great pleasure from the favoured position he enjoyed at Windsor, and the intimacy he had with the King, Queen and Princesses. 'Wyatt considers the Queen a very warm friend of his ... [and] is always treated with great respect at Windsor.' Before long he was living at the Castle in the apartments once occupied by Sir Christopher Wren and dining at the Equerries' table with the Lord Chamberlain. When the architect could not be found in his office in London, his clerks and frustrated clients always knew that they could track him down at Windsor.

A letter from Princess Elizabeth to Wyatt survives, written on pretty neo-classical paper:

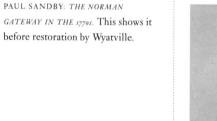

PAUL SANDBY: *THE NORMAN GATEWAY IN THE 1770s.* This shows it before restoration by Wyatville.

JOHN WOOTTON: *FREDERICK, PRINCE OF WALES, IN THE HUNTING FIELD.* Frederick was keen on hunting in Windsor Great Park, as was his son George III, and it was this and the beauty of the landscape which initially attracted the King and determined him to restore Windsor as his principal country palace.

GIULIO CLOVIO, *c.* 1530. This splendid Italian sixteenth-century illuminated manuscript was acquired for the Royal Library by George III.

CANALETTO: *THE THAMES FROM THE TERRACE OF SOMERSET HOUSE*, *c.* 1750. One of the Canalettos acquired with the Consul Smith Collection. George III extended the Royal Collection by acquiring en bloc the paintings of Joseph Smith, the English Consul in Venice. Smith's collection included over forty works by Canaletto. Many of the Canalettos in the Royal Collection were hung in the Grand Corridor at Windsor by George IV.

Princess Elizabeth thinks it right to inform Mr Wyatt that the King named him as wishing to see him two or three times yesterday saying he had some money matters to settle ... The Queen thinks the most agreeable time for His Majesty to see Mr Wyatt will be at Windsor – either Saturday or Sunday.

By an odd chance the tone but not the actual words of a conversation between George III and James Wyatt has been preserved in John Galt's novel *Sir Andrew Wylie*. Galt bases an encounter between his Scottish hero and the King on a conversation he had overheard between James Wyatt and George III on a visit to Windsor Castle. Galt and his friends had climbed into the scaffolding of the new Great Staircase to inspect the work when the King and the architect came in:

The King observed us, particularly myself who was so conspicuous, and lingered with Mr Wyatt until he had satisfied his curiosity by looking at us; speaking all the time ... and looking about as he was speaking. It was evident that he spoke more at random than seriously addressed the architect, being occupied in noticing us. Something in his manner drew my attention and from that interview which lasted probably several minutes, I caught a durable remembrance of his peculiarities – I can see him still.

*

Work began on the Castle in 1800 and continued until the King's final illness in 1811 brought the whole project to a halt in a part-finished state, though over £150,000 had been spent. George III's interest in Windsor in middle age was prompted by his political outlook and the impact on it of national circumstances. He was a 'natural conservative' and instinctively revered ancient institutions such as the Church and the monarchy. Such views had made him unpopular at the beginning of his reign in the face of the radical MP John Wilkes, who had stirred up a popular campaign for Liberty, and the loss of the American colonies, but the French Revolution changed all that. The overthrow of the traditional structure of society across the Channel provoked a strong feeling of revulsion in England and fuelled the High Tory reaction of the influential orator, Edmund Burke, and Prime Minister William Pitt, suddenly making the King and all he symbolized extremely popular as the embodiment of English tradition. At the same time attitudes towards the Middle Ages changed, as people wished to emphasize traditional values and the continuity of English institutions. Thus

CANALETTO: *A REGATTA ON THE GRAND CANAL*, c. 1733.

Windsor, the ancient seat of the monarchy, came to have a special significance for the King. George III, who in his youth under Chambers' guidance had been a dyed-in-the-wool Palladian, found himself moved by Windsor's associational qualities and became an enthusiastic convert to Gothic, which he saw as the ancient, English, national style as opposed to modern Italian-derived classical architecture. He wrote to his daughter, the Duchess of Wurtemberg, in 1803:

> *I never thought I should have adopted Gothic instead of Grecian Architecture, but the bad taste of the last fifty years has so entirely corrupted the professors of the latter. I have taken to the former from thinking Wyatt perfect in that style.*

As well as restoring St George's Chapel in the 1780s and the 1790s under the direction of Henry Emlyn, the King had made some alterations to the state rooms with the help of John Yenn, the architect-pupil of Sir William Chambers. The King's Audience Chamber

CHARLES WILD: *THE KING'S AUDIENCE CHAMBER.* George III remodelled this room to make a Garter Throne Room. The canopy was decorated with floral needlework by Mrs Pawsey and the walls hung with large canvases commissioned from Benjamin West depicting Edward III and the Black Prince.

had been modernized in 1786, when a new marble chimneypiece was inserted and the walls hung with Garter-blue velvet trimmed with floral needlework borders designed by Mary Moser and worked by Mrs Pawsey's school of needlework. The canopy of state over the new throne had matching needlework and was supported by painted pilasters designed by Benjamin West and executed by Biagio Rebecca. This approach set the theme for the work in the state rooms, which consisted of replacing dark wainscots with brighter damask and bolection chimneypieces with more elaborate designs of sculpted statuary marble, but generally retaining the old panelled dado, Gibbons' carved cornices, and repairing Verrio's painted ceilings.

Benjamin West was George III's favourite artist and was much patronized by him in the early part of his reign. West had been born near Pennsylvania but travelled and studied in Italy between 1760 and 1763. In Rome he had come under the influence of Anton Raphael Mengs and Gavin Hamilton, from whom he had learnt to paint history pictures. In 1763 he settled in London and began to exhibit his paintings, soon coming to the notice of George III, who commissioned a series of heroic canvases from him for the Warm Room at Buckingham House; he was appointed Historical Painter to George III in 1772. He was an important figure in the team of artists and designers employed at Windsor. He painted a large series of canvases for a proposed chapel to be built in the Horn Court which never materialized. These paintings were devoted to the theme of 'Revealed Religion'. He was employed on the redecoration of the King's Audience Chamber which George III envisaged as a Garter Throne Room, where new companions of the Order could be installed. West's programme there consisted of eight large canvases illustrating the life of Edward III and hung in a chrono-logical arrangement on the walls: *Edward III Forcing the Passing of the River Somme in France*; *Edward III Embracing his Son, the Black Prince, on the Field of Battle at Crécy*; *Queen Philippa Defeats David, King of Scotland at Nevill's Cross and Takes Him Prisoner*; *Queen Philippa Asking Edward III to Spare St Pierre and the Brave Burgesses of Calais*; *Edward III Crowning Ribemont at Calais*; *The Inauguration of the Most Noble Order of the Garter*; *Edward, the Black Prince, Receiving John King of France and His Son as Prisoners*; and *St George Slaying the Dragon*. For these West was paid the large sum of £6,930. George IV disliked West's religious paintings, some of which were later sold and are no longer part of the Royal Collection. But the subjects of the original commission

GEORGE STUBBS: *THE PRINCE OF WALES'S PHAETON*, 1793.

give a very clear idea of George III's attitude to Windsor, his appreciation of its historic associations and his wish to restore and enhance its traditions and historical significance.

James Wyatt seemed to be the designer ideally suited to give architectural expression to these ideals. Though he had risen to fame as a fashionable purveyor of a refined Adamesque classical manner, from early in his career he had been interested in Gothic architecture and it was as a performer in the Gothic style that he attained a special celebrity among his contemporaries. He told the King, in excuse for his early work, that 'there had been no regular architecture since Sir William Chambers – that when he came from Italy he found the public taste corrupted by the Adams, and he was obliged to comply with it.' Brilliant but unprincipled, Wyatt could design whatever was demanded of him.

All Georgian architects were called upon from time to time to produce designs in the medieval manner where circumstances seemed to demand it, for instance at Oxford or the ancient cathedrals, but though Wyatt was not a Gothic innovator, he did it better than any of his predecessors. This was partly because he had a better knowledge of authentic medieval prototypes, especially Perpendicular examples, than any of his rivals displayed, and partly because he was able to capture some of the picturesque irregularity and spatial drama of medieval architecture, which appealed to the late Georgian sensibility. In Horace Walpole's view, Wyatt's work revived 'the long-forgotten beauties of Gothic architecture'.

Wyatt's new Staircase at Windsor was a spatial *tour de force*, as well as being reasonably accurate in its deployment of Gothic detail. It replaced the Queen's Great Staircase by Hugh May, and like its predecessor it rose on axis from the Grand Entrance and the Quadrangle. A low-vaulted vestibule supported by clustered piers of correct Perpendicular section led to a long straight flight of stone steps under a tall vaulted space lit from an octagonal lantern nearly 100 ft (30.5 m) above ground level. All the stucco work in this soaring space was executed by Francis Bernasconi, who was paid in 1805 for 'Gothic elliptical arches, elliptical soffits, Gothic comp mouldings, enriched spandrels, the Royal Arms, angels with plainshields, etc.' Although the Staircase was later removed by Wyatville, Bernasconi's vaulted ceiling with its Gothic mouldings and angels survives in the Grand Vestibule today.

Bernasconi was a craftsman much employed by the Wyatts. He is thought to have been the son of Bernato Bernasconi, a poor Italian

THE GRAND VESTIBULE CEILING AND LANTERN. This soaring fan vault was designed by James Wyatt as part of his Gothic restoration of the Upper Ward for George III. The plaster was executed by Francis Bernasconi, a stuccoist of genius who also worked at Buckingham Palace.

JAMES STEPHANOFF: *THE QUEEN'S BEDCHAMBER*, c. 1819. George III carefully preserved Verrio's painted ceilings.

immigrant who had worked as a plasterer at Claydon, Buckinghamshire, for Lord Verney. Francis was employed by Wyatt on a wide range of houses in London and the country, and he did much work in the royal palaces: at Carlton House and Buckingham Palace as well as at Windsor, where he continued to be employed in the next reign by James Wyatt's nephew Jeffry Wyatville. The choice of the rest of Wyatt's team showed a degree of nepotism, as they comprised his younger son Matthew Cotes Wyatt and his cousin Edward Wyatt as decorative painter and wood-carver respectively.

Matthew Cotes Wyatt had been educated at Eton but showed an aptitude for drawing and painting, so his father recommended him to the King to repair the Verrio ceilings in place of John François Rigaud, who had extended the Queen's State Bed Chamber ceiling with a scene of Diana and Jupiter. Though only twenty-two years old, and with no previous artistic experience, Matthew was appointed to do this prestigious work. As well as general touching up and refurbishment, the commission consisted of replacing some of the ceilings in Verrio's style. It occupied him for the best part of seven years. The artist and connoisseur Sir Francis Bourgeois was incensed that, for this important work, worth about £4,000, James Wyatt had chosen his own son, 'a young inexperienced artist ... to the exclusion of artists of known ability'. Bourgeois and the Royal Academician Joseph Farington both considered Matthew Cotes Wyatt totally inadequate for the occasion. The painter Sir William Beechey, on the other hand, thought 'his ceilings at Windsor ... would do honour to any artist.' As Wyatville destroyed them it is not possible for us to judge.

Matthew Cotes Wyatt restored Verrio's work in St George's Hall and painted a new ceiling in the lantern of the King's Guard Chamber. He also designed a 'rich ceiling' for the new Blenheim Tower on the north front but it was not executed and the tower never finished.

In 1804 James Wyatt enlarged the King's Closet and Matthew Cotes Wyatt painted entirely new ceilings there and in the adjoining Dressing Room depicting St George and the Dragon. He was also employed to paint a series of twenty-eight historical full-length portraits of Knights of the Garter. These were intended as part of a scheme for converting the dismal old Lady Chapel or Tomb House in the Lower Ward into a Garter Chapter House, a project which was never completed; only twenty-one were painted and they have been destroyed.

Edward Wyatt, like Bernasconi, was also employed at Carlton House, and later at Buckingham Palace, as a carver and gilder. At Windsor he carefully copied the Grinling Gibbons cornices in the state rooms where they needed to be repaired or where rooms were extended, such as the Queen's State Bed Chamber, which James Wyatt doubled in size in 1804 by taking in the Closet and an adjoining staircase. For the Queen's Audience Chamber, Edward Wyatt carved a 'rich frize emblemmatically describing two of the Elements, Land and Water', which still survives in store. Such was the quality of his work that it is difficult to tell it apart from the seventeenth-century originals by Grinling Gibbons. Like Bernasconi, Edward Wyatt continued to work at the Castle in the next reign under Jeffry Wyatville.

The general aim of George III and James Wyatt was to transform the exterior of the buildings in the Upper Ward into a Gothic palace, while retaining the character of the Hugh May state rooms. Wyatt started at the west end of the State Apartments, gothicizing the Star Building by adding battlements and turrets. Both here and on the east and south sides of the Quadrangle, where new private

CHARLES WILD: *KING'S BEDCHAMBER*, *c.* 1819. George III modernized the state rooms by removing the oak wainscot from the walls, apart from the dado, and substituting crimson damask to make a richer background for the paintings.

CHARLES WILD: *THE QUEEN'S DRAWING ROOM*, *c.* 1819. George III redecorated and refurnished Charles II's State Apartments, as can be seen in this room with its up-to-date chairs and stools.

apartments were contrived for Queen Charlotte and her children, Hugh May's windows were replaced with pointed Gothic ones (discernible from Wyatville's by the use of white Portland stone tracery). The internal communications were also improved by a double-decker cloister, built round the Horn Court on the model of Wilton, Wiltshire, and by a new grand entrance from the Quadrangle, which was lowered two feet by excavating the surface. Inside the north block a suite of plain private apartments was formed for George III on the ground floor, and there he was confined during the melancholy years of his illness, the sentries pacing the terrace outside saluting when they saw his wild unshaven

CANALETTO: *BACINO DI S. MARCO ON ASCENSION DAY c. 1733–4.*

THOMAS GAINSBOROUGH: *JOHANN CHRISTIAN FISCHER, c. 1780.* George III and Queen Charlotte did not like Sir Joshua Reynolds but were great patrons of Gainsborough, acquiring many portraits by him.

face staring blankly out of the window. Wyatt's Grand Staircase provided a ceremonial access to the State Apartments and was given a handsome balustrade of bronzed ironwork with polished brass ornament. The Charles II State Apartments on the first floor were discreetly altered and some of them enlarged, but keeping to their existing style.

The new ceilings painted by John François Rigaud and Matthew Cotes Wyatt were in a neo-baroque manner similar to Verrio's, just as Edward Wyatt's carving mimicked Grinling Gibbons. Edward Wyatt also repaired some of the old furniture. Unfortunately this sympathetic conservationist approach to the Charles II apartments did not extend into the next reigns when Wyatville modernized all except three of the old ensembles and replaced the painted ceilings with somewhat commonplace designs of gilded stucco which survive today. The rooms as redecorated and furnished by George III were recorded in Pyne's *Royal Residences*, published in 1819, for which the original watercolours by Charles Wild are in the Royal Library at Windsor.

As well as the work to the State Apartments, George III also restored the Tomb House east of St George's Chapel in the Lower Ward. He formed a large new burial vault underneath and fitted up the Chapel interior with a plaster Gothic vault and Matthew Cotes Wyatt's paintings, to form a chapter house for the Order of the Garter. George III's conservative, historicist, even reverential approach to

ANNIBALE CARRACCI: *SELF-PORTRAIT, c. 1575.*

MICHELANGELO: *THE RISEN CHRIST,* c. 1530. George III added considerably to the Royal Collection, in particular to the incomparable collection of Old Master drawings which are the single most important treasure of the Royal Library.

HANS HOLBEIN: *SIR JOHN MORE*,
c. 1527-8.

LEONARD DA VINCI: *STAR OF*
BETHLEHEM, c. 1505-7.

ALBRECHT DÜRER: *GREYHOUND*,
c. 1500.

Windsor is revealed in Pyne's remarks about the bed in the King's State Bedroom: 'Queen Anne's bed which being valued by his present Majesty is preserved with care, having a crimson curtain to draw over it, and it is guarded from the rude approach of idle curiosity by a screen in front.' So highly did the King value this relic that he 'would not displace [it] for the most splendid bed in the universe'.

As part of the mystique of Windsor, the King designed a special Windsor uniform to be worn by gentlemen when at court in the Castle; of blue cloth with red and gold facings, it is still worn on occasion at Windsor today. In April 1805 he revived the ceremony of the installation of Knights of the Garter, for which event St George's Hall was fitted with an organ and music gallery, and its wall paintings were cleaned and restored. Though the King was increasingly stirred by the historic and chivalric associations of Windsor, Queen Charlotte was far less enthusiastic about the Castle and wrote to a friend in 1804:

> We are now returned to our new habitation in the castle. Not to shock you ... with my opinion on this subject I will briefly tell you that I have changed from a very comfortable and warm habitation to the coldest house, rooms and passages that ever existed.

As well as employing Henry Emlyn, James Wyatt, Benjamin West and their team of craftsmen to restore both St George's Chapel and the Tomb House in the Lower Ward and the state rooms in the Upper Ward, George III added considerably to the collection of works of art. In the earlier years of his reign, the cream of his acquisitions was displayed at Buckingham House in London, but after he made Windsor his principal country house he moved some of the works of art there, and other parts of his collections were concentrated at Windsor by his successors. The single most important acquisition of his reign was the purchase in 1762 of the collection formed in Venice by the British Consul there, Joseph Smith. This included a large group of works by Venetian artists, including over forty by Canaletto, most of which are now at Windsor, the majority of them having been hung in the Grand Corridor by George IV. The spectacular collection of Old Master, mainly Italian, drawings which is the single greatest treasure of the Royal Collection, was also greatly enhanced by George III, and since the reign of William IV has been housed in the Royal Library at Windsor.

George III's father, Frederick, Prince of Wales, who died young

CHAPTER FOUR

GEORGE IV

Romantic Revival

George IV, who succeeded to the throne in 1820, was the major patron of the arts of the Hanoverian dynasty, exceeding both his father George III and grandfather Frederick, Prince of Wales, in the scale and quality of his building and collecting; it is almost entirely due to him that the English monarchy today has any palaces worthy of the name. Reacting against the simple domesticity of his father's life, he set about providing himself with settings suited to the 'monarch of the richest and most powerful nation in the world'. At Windsor he created a Romantic feudal pile grander than anything of the kind in existence; at Buckingham Palace he contrived an elegant, Francophile royal residence which goes some way towards filling the gap caused by the loss of Westminster and Whitehall Palaces; and at Brighton he erected one of the last as well as one of the most extravagant and certainly the most exotic of those casinos or pavilions which had been such a delightful feature of eighteenth-century royal building in Europe.

In retrospect, George IV's building activity can be seen to have formed three main phases of increasing magnificence, reflecting his political position. When young, he was satisfied with elegant Louis XVI rooms of exquisite restraint as a civilized setting for his comparatively carefree existence at Carlton House and Brighton Pavilion. On becoming Regent in middle age, he found that he needed grander settings for a more formal court and for official business – extra state rooms as well as rooms for audiences and council meetings; this had brought about an extensive remodelling of Carlton House and the enlargement and reconstruction of Brighton Pavilion, as well as the creation of a commodious country house, the Royal Lodge in Windsor Great Park. Finally, on succeed-

SIR THOMAS LAWRENCE:
GEORGE IV, Coronation portrait, 1821.

The Prince's revulsion from France brought about by the excesses of the Revolution was short-lived, but it had important side-effects on his architectural patronage. It was one of the reasons for his switch from French decoration to oriental at Brighton Pavilion. In 1797 *The Times* reported with approval that the Prince intended to dismiss all Frenchmen from his service and expressed the hope that every nobleman would follow his example. In fact the Prince did not carry out this threat, and it was with a certain irony that he complained to Lady Bessborough that 'there was such a cry against French things etc., that he was afraid of his furniture being accus'd of Jacobinism.'

This hiatus marked a change in the character of George IV's Francophilia. In early life he had identified himself with the more progressive elements in contemporary French life, but in later years it was to the Grand Siècle that he looked back with nostalgia, and he modelled himself and his rooms on Louis XIV and Louis XV. The so-called 'Louis Quatorze' style with its Boulle, rococo, ormolu and lashings of gilt, rather than the simpler elegance of the style purveyed by the architect Henry Holland, the painter Louis Pernotin and the furniture-maker Georges Jacob, was to be expressed in the new rooms at Windsor Castle.

George IV had a great sense of style and feeling for occasion. When he opened Parliament in state it was with an almost theatrical flair, while his Coronation, in which all the participants wore specially designed 'Tudor' dress, was the grandest in post-Reformation English history. In creating a setting for his court, it was to Versailles and the Tuileries that he looked for inspiration. His purchase of French works of art was partly an attempt to recreate for his own receptions an ambience similar to that which had provided the background to the ritual of the old court of France. In his youth he had bought contemporary French furniture from Paris through fashionable dealers like Dominique Daguerre, but with the systematic dispersal of the contents of the French royal palaces by the revolutionaries, he was able to secure many earlier masterpieces of French eighteenth-century furniture as well as the Dutch cabinet paintings which were their fashionable accompaniment. For these later purchases he relied heavily on members of his household acting as his agents, including Louis Weltje, his cook, and François Benois, his confectioner. At a higher social level, several courtiers and members of the 'Carlton House set' who were keenly interested in art and architecture acted as advisers to the King on matters of

taste. Chief of these was Sir Charles Long, later Lord Farnborough, the *éminence grise* behind much of George IV's activity as a connoisseur of art and patron of architecture. Long, for example, vetted many of the King's more important purchases of works of art, travelling to Paris on occasion for this purpose, and was directly responsible for supervising the schemes of restoration and decoration adopted at St James's Palace, Windsor Castle and Buckingham Palace in the 1820s.

George IV transformed Windsor Castle into the principal seat of the English monarchy at a cost of about a million pounds. Almost as soon as his father was dead, he started to plan moving to the Castle from the Royal Lodge, the overgrown *cottage orné* which he had built in the middle of the Great Park when he was Prince Regent.

In 1823 he closed the terraces, to secure more privacy, and moved into the Castle, but having more luxurious tastes than his father he soon found it uninhabitable without a `major remodelling'. An approach to the Treasury met a favourable response and £150,000 was immediately pledged for the work. A small parliamentary committee including the Chancellor of the Exchequer and Sir

MARTIN-ELOI LIGNEREUX: EGYPTIAN STYLE EBONY AND ORMOLU CABINET WITH *PIETRA DURA* PANELS AND PORPHYRY TOP, 1803, acquired for George IV in Paris by Sir Harry Featherstonhaugh.

Charles Long was set up to supervise it.

Charles Long played the key role in this. He suggested holding a limited competition in 1823 for the reconstruction of the Castle. The architects invited to take part were John Nash, Sir John Soane, and Sir Robert Smirke (the leaders of the architectural profession who were all attached to the Office of Works) together with Jeffry Wyatt (the nephew and pupil of James who had taken over part of his uncle's business). Long drew up a detailed programme for the restoration which he sent to Lord Liverpool, the Prime Minister, before any architect was chosen:

I will state shortly and generally what has occurred to me upon the subject.

Approach
It is almost obvious that the principal Approach to the Castle should be by continuing a direct Line from the magnificent Avenue called the Long Walk to the Court of the Castle itself. It would be desirable that the Court should be entered through a Gothic Arch; and the continuance of the same line would lead directly to the doors of Entrance to the State Apartments ...

External Appearance
The Character of this Castle should be that of simplicity and grandeur, as well as from its History, as from the imposing style of Building belonging to that period, I should say the period of Edward the 3rd is that which should generally predominate, not however excluding the Edifices of earlier periods, where we find anything of grand or picturesque effect — Conway, Carnarvon, Harlech, Ragland, Bodiham, Haddon, and many others, will furnish most useful Examples ...

With respect to particular external Alterations, I will point out one or two which I think would be desirable. In an old Castle there should be some predominant feature, and the Keep seems to furnish such a feature in Windsor Castle. At present there are small Towers rising from the Castle as high as the principal Tower of the Keep. I would add to this tower 20 or 30 feet, carrying it up of the same dimensions as the present tower — a smaller Tower rising out of the present would destroy its dignity and grandeur. This elevated Tower seen from a distance would much improve the general effect of the whole Building ...

I would recommend also, both with a view to external appearance and internal Comfort, that there should be a Corridor in the interior Court on the South and East sides.

FRANÇOIS RÉMOND: PATINATED AND GILT BRONZE LOUIS XVI CANDELABRA, 1783. One of the array of superlative French objects and furnishings acquired for Windsor Castle by George IV in the 1820s.

SIR THOMAS LAWRENCE. *SIR JEFFRY WYATVILLE*, 1829, with his plans for Windsor Castle. Jeffry Wyatt was the nephew of James Wyatt and medievalized his surname when he was knighted by George IV for his restoration of the Castle.

In the event Soane withdrew from the competition, though he prepared a series of splendid survey plans of the Castle, now in the Soane Museum; Nash was given the job of rebuilding Buckingham Palace and only Smirke and Wyatt produced designs for Windsor. Of these, Wyatt's were preferred and he got the job. As a reward for his work at Windsor he was later knighted and medievalized his surname to Wyatville, partly to differentiate himself from all his architect uncles, cousins and nephews. (For the sake of clarity he is referred to here as Wyatville throughout.)

Long's suggestions were all adopted and carried out more or less exactly. The Round Tower was raised 30 ft (9.15 m). George III's Queen's Lodge on the south side of the Castle was demolished and the vista from the Long Walk continued for the first time to the Castle where the George IV Gateway was formed to make the principal entrance. The Grand Corridor was added round the east and south sides of the Quadrangle to improve the internal

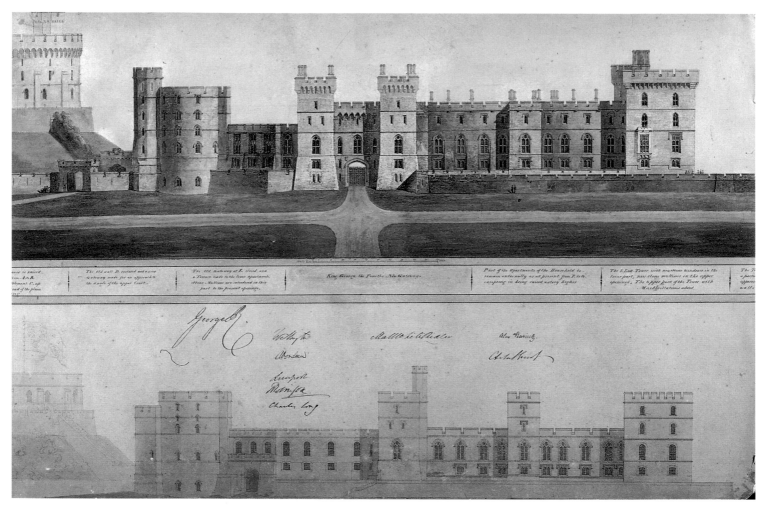

communications. All the external façades of the Upper Ward were made consistently Gothic; towers were heightened for picturesque effect, battlements added and all the windows filled with Gothic tracery. Whereas James Wyatt used white Portland stone, Wyatville used yellow Bath stone. Some of his detail seems rather insensitive, with clumsy machicolations, black galleted pointing and coarse mouldings, but the overall effect is spectacular, particularly the silhouette when seen from the Great Park to the south or from the M4 motorway to the north and east. The skyline composes perfectly from any angle; George IV's castle is a picturesque masterpiece. It was greatly admired by contemporaries. Sir Walter Scott noted in his journal in 1826 that Wyatville possessed 'a great deal of taste and feeling for the Gothic architecture'. Prince Pückler-Muskau, who visited the Castle the following year, wrote: 'All the recent additions are ... so perfectly executed that they are hardly to be distinguished from the old part.'

Wyatville continued and completed James Wyatt's work on the

SIR JEFFRY WYATVILLE: design for the South Front of the Upper Ward, 'before and after'. It shows the proposed new George IV Gateway, and is signed by the King, the architect and the Parliamentary Commissioners for overseeing the reconstruction of the Castle.

SIR JEFFRY WYATVILLE: design for the south and east sides of the Quadrangle, 'before and after', showing the addition of the Grand Corridor as suggested by Charles Long.

north side of the Upper Ward, adding King George IV's Tower with a new entrance from the North Terrace to improve the silhouette of the Star Building; completing the Blenheim Tower which he renamed the George III Tower and is now the Cornwall Tower; and adding a completely new, taller, octagonal tower at the east end called the Brunswick Tower, which makes an effective termination to the overall composition on this side. The east front retains an evenly balanced, almost Georgian character with its four regularly spaced square towers of Henry II date (now called the Prince of Wales Tower, Chester Tower, Clarence Tower and Victoria Tower) but is embellished with machicolations, heavier battlements and a variety of projecting bay windows, the latter being a feature required by George IV, who admired the spatial effect of a bow window in a rectangular room. In front of the eastern range, a sunken private garden was made by building a semi-polygonal raised terrace all round it like a huge bastion or outwall. Underneath part of this was an orangery, containing orange trees given by Louis

GEORGE IV GATEWAY. This was formed by Wyatville at the suggestion of Sir Charles Long (later Lord Farnborough) to form the main entrance from the Long Walk to the Upper Ward.

XVIII of France. On the south side of the Castle, Wyatville completed James Wyatt's refenestration and added more effective battlements. The new George IV Gateway in the centre was created by duplicating the medieval York Tower with the matching Lancaster Tower on the west side of the new archway to create an impressive symmetrical gatehouse precisely on axis with Charles II's Long Walk.

Inside the Quadrangle, the east and south sides were masked by the two-storeyed corridor extension which helped to emphasize the predominance of the three-storeyed northern range. This was further enhanced by enlarging the State Entrance with a projecting *porte-cochère* in a square tower which was both practical and impressive. In niches over the archway were placed statues of Edward III and the Black Prince carved by Richard Westmacott (copied from the effigies on their tombs at Westminster Abbey and Canterbury Cathedral). Above this a clock was framed with the inscription *'Georgius IIII Rex Anno Domini 1827'*.

The George IV Gateway is curiously understated on the Quadrangle side where the Grand Corridor runs over it at

JOSEPH NASH: *THE EAST FRONT* with the sunken garden in 1848.

THE EAST FRONT OF THE UPPER WARD. The basic form with projecting square towers dates back to Henry II's time, but this range was completely remodelled by Wyatville for George IV to contain magnificent and comfortable new royal apartments on the site of the rooms he had occupied when Prince of Wales. The garden was also made for the King; the East Terrace was closed to the public to ensure his privacy.

first-floor level with no particular emphasis. Wyatville contrived a new canted entrance, the Sovereign's Entrance in the southeast corner, leading to the royal apartments. The equestrian statue of Charles II was moved from the centre of the Quadrangle to the foot of the motte, where Wyatville designed a new tall granite plinth for it, incorporating Grinling Gibbons's carved marble panels.

UPPER WARD: detail of Westmacott's statue of Edward III over the State Entrance. It is derived from the King's Tomb in Westminster Abbey.

THE QUADRANGLE as remodelled by Wyatville.

The internal remodelling of the Upper Ward was spectacular as the reconstruction of the exterior, though here Wyatville was given less of a free hand. George IV combined his father's romantic architectural enthusiasm for Windsor with his mother's more practical feeling for comfort. He decided to live not in the north range which his father had occupied, but in new rooms on the sunnier east and south sides of the Castle where his mother and sisters had had their apartments and where he himself had occupied a suite of rooms forty years before. Here he contrived an entirely new royal residence with private rooms, guest rooms and rooms for entertainment within the ancient shell, all tied together by Wyatville's Grand Corridor.

While Wyatville was responsible for the planning and some of the architectural detail of these new rooms, much of the decoration was

THE ENTRANCE TO THE STATE APARTMENTS FROM THE QUADRANGLE, designed by Wyatville. The statues in niches of Edward III and the Black Prince were carved by Richard Westmacott.

the largest furniture-making business in London.

Morel & Seddon were responsible for supplying all the new furniture, copying existing pieces to make pairs or sets, and altering and restoring older pieces in the Royal Collection as well as the numerous examples of French furniture which George IV was buying in these years. They also supplied gilded frames, silk for the walls, the curtains and upholstery. The total cost of their contract between 1825 and 1830 came to over £270,000.

It was under the aegis of Morel & Seddon that the fifteen-year-old boy-genius A. W. N. Pugin was employed to design the Gothic furniture and fittings for the new Dining Room and other Gothic interiors. In some autobiographical jottings Pugin noted on 26 June 1827:

MOREL & SEDDON: DESIGN FOR THE KING'S BEDROOM with Empire-style tent hangings of blue silk.

MOREL & SEDDON: DESIGN FOR THE WINDOW WALL OF THE LIBRARY, now the Green Drawing Room in the royal apartments at Windsor Castle.

Went to design and make working drawings for the gothic furniture of Windsor Castle at £1.1s per day for the following rooms. The Long Gallery, the coffee room, the vestibule anti-room, halls, grand staircase, octagon room in the Brunswick tower, and Great Dining Room.

Pugin later disowned this juvenilia:

everything is crocketed with angular projections, inumerable mitres, sharp ornaments, and turreted extremities ... I have perpetrated many of these enormities in furniture I designed some years ago for Windsor Castle ... all my Knowledge of Pointed Architecture was confined to a tolerably good notion of details in the abstract; but these I employed with so little judgement or propriety, that although the parts were correct and exceedingly well executed, collectively they appeared a complete burlesque of pointed design.

Pugin was being unnecessarily severe. It is the ingenious combination of scholarly detail and exotic materials in original compositions which makes his Windsor furniture so visually satisfying. Much of it survives at Windsor, including the chairs in the State Entrance, benches in the Grand Corridor and side tables in the dining rooms.

At Windsor the sequence of Gothic rooms within the Castle reflected the external architecture and the history of the building. Generally speaking the aim was to make the entry and processional spaces – including the principal staircases – and the eating rooms Gothic, while fitting out the drawing rooms and royal apartments in a version of George IV's favourite Francophile manner. But this juxtaposition of Gothic and classical was not peculiar to Windsor. Already at Carlton House George IV had contrived a Gothic conservatory, Gothic dining room and Gothic library in that otherwise impeccably neo-classical palace. Gothic was an aspect of his taste, and one which found a perfect outlet at Windsor.

Altogether the new royal apartments at Windsor were Carlton House writ large; they represented its recreation on a larger scale, containing many of the same fixtures, fittings and furnishings. When George IV acceded to the throne in 1820 and decided to move from Carlton House to Buckingham Palace, his intention was to divide the contents of Carlton House between the new Buckingham Palace and the new royal apartments at Windsor. As early as 1824 Charles Long had attended the King to discuss the disposition of the Carlton House things in the Castle. Detailed inventories, pictorial records and drawings were made so that these chattels, the result of

MOREL & SEDDON: OAK STOOL IN THE GRAND CORRIDOR. The fifteen-year-old Pugin helped with the designs of the Gothic furniture for the Gothic rooms at Windsor, including the State Dining Room, Coffee Room and Grand Corridor.

Bernasconi, but otherwise are a combination of elements from Carlton House. The crisply carved door trophies by Edward Wyatt in the Great Drawing Room came from the Blue Velvet Room, and the black marble and bronze chimneypiece (by B.L. Vulliamy) from the Crimson Drawing Room. The bookcases in the Library came from the Golden Drawing Room, though more were made up by Morel & Seddon to match.

JOSEPH NASH: THE GREEN DRAWING ROOM. The magnificent suite of royal apartments in the east range of the Upper Ward expressed George IV's Francophile tastes at their most sumptuous and contained many fixtures from his demolished London palace, Carlton House, including the bookcases, doors and chimneypiece here. This was intended by George IV as a library.

The more private rooms comprising guest rooms in the south range, the Queen's Sitting Room, Bed Room and Dressing Room in the Victoria Tower, and the King's Bed Room, Dressing Room, Bathroom, Sitting Room and Secretary's Room in the east wing, also contained chimneypieces and other fixtures from Carlton House. The whole sequence from the Victoria Tower to the State Dining Room is the finest and most complete example in existence of late Georgian taste.

In addition to the furniture brought from Carlton House or supplied by Morel & Seddon, George IV acquired many superb pieces of French furniture specially for Windsor Castle in Paris or London sales in the 1820s. Many of these were on a larger scale than the furniture acquired for the smaller rooms of Carlton House. In 1825, for instance, he had bought several Louis XIV Boulle pieces in Paris. In 1826 he commissioned directly in Paris a gilt bronze mounted pedestal for an equestrian statue of Louis XIV which he placed in the Dining Room in 1828, for which the craftsmen were the sons-in-law and successors of P.-P. Thomire, A.A. Beauvisage and L.A.C. Carbonelle. In the 1820s his purchases, doubtless with Windsor in mind, included the four massive Caffieri candelabra incorporating patinated bronzes of the seasons by Desjardins, which came from the collection of the Comte d'Orsay; the Comtesse de Provence's jewel cabinet by J.-H. Riesener, now in the White Drawing Room, and the three great Boulle armoires, now in the Grand Corridor. The jewel cabinet and other magnificent pieces were acquired by the King specially for Windsor at George Watson Taylor's sale in 1828. So spectacular, and expensive, was this purchase that he felt that he had to justify himself in a letter to his Prime Minister, the Duke of Wellington, in February 1828:

FRANÇOIS GIRARDON: EQUESTRIAN BRONZE STATUE OF LOUIS XIV, c. 1700 This was one of a number of superb French works of art acquired by George IV specially for Windsor Castle in the 1820s. The ebonized base with ormolu mounts was made for him in Paris in 1826.

Private. I write for the purpose of communicating with you on the subject of Windsor Castle, Buckingham Palace etc., etc. It has been clearly explain'd to me what your intentions are on all the points. I understand that you will ask for a further grant this year of one hundred and fifty thousand pounds to be appropriated to Windsor Castle. This is very satisfactory to my feelings. Pray guard the Chancellor of the Exchequer, against making any promise in the House that Windsor Castle will not require a further grant, as I fear that this sum will not complete it. Not the slightest alteration has ever been made in the original plan of architecture, and the additional expense incurr'd has entirely arisen from the age of the Castle. God knows, at my time of life, the nation has a much greater interest in this Royal edifice than I can have, but I should be truly sorry not to see it completed. I find that the Commissioners are embarassed respecting the ormolu furniture which I thought it right to have bought under the circumstances of Mr Watson Taylor's sale; it is quite appropriate for Windsor Castle, and worth double what it cost, but, my friend, who manages my private affairs, will from some fund or other relieve the Commission from this expense. I may however, as well take this opportunity of observing that there is now already in Windsor Castle twenty thousand pounds worth of my own private property, the estimate of which is now at the Treasury, and this was made under the cognizance of the present Chancellor.

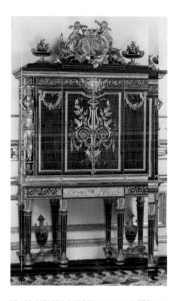

JEAN-HENRI RIESENER: THE JEWEL CABINET OF THE COMTESSE DE PROVENCE. Made for her apartment at Versailles in 1785, it was acquired by George IV for Windsor where it adorns the White Drawing Room.

The Grand Corridor, designed by Wyatville and stretching 550 ft (167.6 m) round two sides of the Quadrangle, was furnished under the King's immediate supervision; in many ways it is the finest surviving expression of his taste. It was intended as a gallery for paintings and sculpture. The walls were stone colour, the ceiling

Gothic room with Bernasconi plasterwork, and to the east to the Waterloo Chamber. This filled the former Horn Court, which was roofed over for the purpose, with a timber-framed ship-like clerestory. It was intended as a top-lit gallery for the series of twenty-five portraits by Sir Thomas Lawrence of the allied sovereigns, statesmen and military commanders who had been responsible for the overthrow of Napoleon. Commissioned in 1814

THE WATERLOO CHAMBER: DETAIL OF THE CEILING. This unusual picture gallery was contrived by Wyatville within Edward III's Horn Court. The design of the ceiling with raking top lighting is reminiscent of a man-o'-war of Nelson's period. The chandeliers were made for Queen Victoria by Osler of Birmingham after the Great Exhibition.

when the King was still Prince Regent, these had taken several years to complete. The project had been George IV's own idea, and it was his most inspired act of contemporary patronage. The proposal to cover over the Horn Court to make a special gallery for their display was Charles Long's, after it had been decided that the portraits would be most appropriate at Windsor.

To the east of the Waterloo Chamber the King's Guard Chamber was enlarged and remodelled to create a ballroom, now known as the Grand Reception Room. This was a *tour de force* of 'Louis Quatorze' decoration, with a rococo plaster ceiling by Bernasconi and convincing *boiseries* on the walls framing Gobelins tapestries. This ensemble had little to do with Wyatville. His assistant Henry Ashton later remarked: 'the introduction of French boiserie ... would never have appeared in the Castle had the architect been solely

SIR THOMAS LAWRENCE: *POPE PIUS VII*, 1819. The array of portraits of the allied statesmen, sovereigns and soldiers responsible for defeating Napoleon, displayed in the Waterloo Chamber at Windsor Castle, was George IV's most audacious piece of contemporary artistic patronage. Lawrence's portrait of the aged Benedictine Pope painted in Rome in 1819 is a masterpiece.

guided by his own judgement.' The conception was George IV's own. The tapestries were among the thirty-six Gobelins tapestries acquired specially for the King in Paris by Charles Long on a visit in 1825. Wood carvings for the *boiseries* were bought from the Parisian dealer Delahante for £500 in 1826 and used as models for Francis Bernasconi to copy in plaster composition. The tall narrow upright panels flanking the tapestries appear to be the original French timber panels, while the matching plaster decoration above and below is by Bernasconi. The details of the room were probably the responsiblity of Frederick and John Crace, decorators of genius who were also responsible for the colouring and gilding.

To the north of the Waterloo Chamber, Wyatville knocked together the old King's Audience Chamber and part of the King's Privy Chamber to make a new larger Throne Room. The most drastic

SIR THOMAS LAWRENCE: *MATVEI IVANOVITCH COUNT PLATOV*, 1814. Platov was responsible for masterminding the campaign which destroyed Napoleon's army in the retreat from Moscow in 1812.

represents Scott's romantic vision of the Middle Ages, its walls adorned with trophies of arms and its ceiling decorated with the shields of all the Knights of the Garter from the foundation of the Order onwards. The heraldic decoration was devised by the antiquary and stained-glass designer Thomas Willement, 'heraldic artist to His Majesty the King', and the author of *Regal Heraldry: the Armorial Insignia of the Kings and Queens of England* (1821).

At the time of the King's death at Windsor Castle in 1830, the fitting-up of the state rooms at Windsor remained incomplete, with

GARTER THRONE ROOM. Detail of ceiling plasterwork designed by Wyatville and executed by Bernasconi. It incorporates the insignia and collar of the Order of the Garter.

the result that they lack some of the *élan* of the eastern enfilade. The remodelling was continued into the next two reigns under Wyatville's and then under Edward Blore's direction, but exuding a dull competence rather than the zest and brio which had invested the work in George IV's lifetime. Many of the Verrio ceilings, for instance, which were found to be in poor condition, were taken down and replaced by heavy gilded plaster designs sporting thick naturalistic scrollwork, Stuart and Hanoverian heraldry and the monograms of William IV and Queen Adelaide. William IV also transferred the Royal Library to Windsor, converting for the purpose the suite of three rooms at the north-western extremity of the State Apartments, including the old Queen's State Bed Chamber and Queen Elizabeth's Gallery.

Many objects commissioned by George IV were only completed after his death or installed by William IV, including Sir Richard

NICOLAUS SCHMIDT: NAUTILUS CUP AND COVER, Nuremburg, late sixteenth century. This luxurious object, acquired by George IV in 1823, came from the Tylney collection at Wanstead House.

SIR PETER PAUL RUBENS: *PORTRAIT OF A WOMAN*, *c.* 1625–30. Bought by George IV when Prince Regent in 1818.

Westmacott's huge equestrian bronze statue of George III, commissioned in 1824 but only erected in 1831 on a tall rocky granite plinth designed by Wyatville at the south end of the Long Walk. George IV's other principal embellishment of the Great Park was the artificial ruin on the banks of Virginia Water, constructed out of genuine Roman columns and architectural fragments from Leptis Magna in modern Libya. These had been sent to the Prince Regent in 1817 as a gift by the Bashaw of Tripoli and were stored at the British Museum. The idea of using these classical fragments to create a picturesque 'Temple of Augustus', seems to have been, like so much else at Windsor, Charles Long's. In August 1824 he wrote to the British Museum (of which he was a Trustee): 'His Majesty commands that the Columns and Fragments deposited in the courtyard of the Museum should be placed at the disposal of his architect Mr Jeffry Wyatt, to whom His Majesty has given further instructions.' A party

CHAPTER FIVE

QUEEN VICTORIA

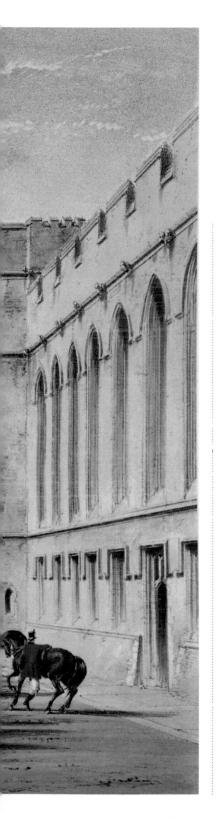

When Queen Victoria came to the throne on 27 June 1837 she found herself in possession of magnificent new palaces both in London and at Windsor, her predecessor, William IV, having finished off all that remained to be done when George IV had died. At Windsor Castle, the reconstruction of the Upper Ward was completed by 1835. The young Queen found in the Upper Ward a magnificently constructed, rationally planned and superbly furnished residence which, apart from minor adjustments, required little further structural work during her reign (or indeed in those of subsequent monarchs down to the later twentieth century). She moved in immediately.

Windsor had happy memories for her of her uncle George IV. As a little girl she had visited him at Royal Lodge and been treated kindly. The King by then was old and fat, swollen with drink, dropsy and drugs, and he used to spend his days secluded from the public gaze, dozing and fishing in the Chinese Fishing Pavilion or driving through the glades in the Great Park in his carriage. 'Give me your little paw,' he had said to the young Princess, helping her into his carriage. And when he had asked what tune she would like his band to play, she had tactfully replied: 'God Save The King'.

In many ways Windsor Castle saw its apogee in the reign of Queen Victoria. She spent the greatest portion of every year at Windsor, and in her reign it enjoyed the position of principal palace of the British monarchy and the focus of the British Empire as well as nearly the whole of royal Europe (many members of which were the Queen's relations and grandchildren). The Castle was visited by sovereigns, ambassadors and ministers from all over the world and was the scene of a series of splendid state visits. On these occasions the state rooms were brought back into use for the royal guests.

JOSEPH NASH: *THE QUADRANGLE* during the state visit of Louis Philippe in 1848.

It is as the 'widow at Windsor' in the second half of her reign that Queen Victoria lives on in the public imagination, moving in her long black dress as if on castors and surrounded by Indian servants dressed in scarlet with striped turbans and sashes – scenes captured in many memoirs and letters by guests and statesmen who awaited the Queen in George IV's Grand Corridor before following her into dinner.

Although Wyatville had left the Castle in such splendid order, comfortable and convenient as well as magnificent, that no major work was required, Queen Victoria did make a few relatively small-scale alterations and adjustments. In the State Apartments, the chief

THE GRAND STAIRCASE, as reconstructed in 1866 by Anthony Salvin for Queen Victoria.

CHARLES WILD: *THE RECEPTION OF NAPOLEON III AND THE EMPRESS EUGENIE AT WINDSOR CASTLE IN APRIL 1855*. This shows Wyatville's staircase before it was altered by Salvin.

of these was the reconstruction of the Grand Staircase. As built by Wyatville this had risen in one central flight from the north-south vestibule of the State Entrance and returned in two flights to a landing and the door to the Grand Vestibule on the first floor. Under Queen Victoria this arrangement was reversed. The old Wyatt entrance vestibule on axis with the State Entrance was closed off, and a new entrance hall created at right angles within Edward III's surviving vaulted undercroft. From this an awkwardly contrived short flight of steps led up to the half-landing, from which a single wider flight now swept up to the Grand Vestibule. This worked well at the upper level where the Staircase is well-lit and looks impressive, but the lower flights, and the indirect connection with the State Entrance could hardly be worse. It is difficult to understand why Wyatville's spacious and lucid arrangement was replaced with a design which is so obviously inferior.

This unnecessary work was done in 1866 and the architect employed was Anthony Salvin, who had already designed various works in the Lower Ward. Following the death of Wyatville, who was buried in St George's Chapel in 1840, Edward Blore had been employed as architect at Windsor, principally on the repair of structures in the Lower Ward. Blore was the son of an antiquarian lawyer and had gained himself a reputation for economy and efficiency at Lambeth Palace and elsewhere. He had been brought in to finish off Nash's work at Buckingham Palace, and on the strength of that, he had been used elsewhere by the royal family and the Commissioners of Works. Between 1840 and 1847 Queen Victoria had employed Blore to convert the polygonal Band Room, between the Great Dining Room and the east end of St George's Hall, into a somewhat constricted private Chapel. This meant that the band had in future to play during meals on the garden terrace outside the Dining Room windows, though there was also a small new band room above the glass pantry adjoining the Dining Room. The new Chapel which resulted was a peculiarly shaped space. It was never much appreciated.

Blore had also restored, in the same years, the houses of the Military Knights on the south side of the Lower Ward, and reconstructed the Salisbury Tower at the south-west corner.

As Blore, however, was not much admired by Prince Albert, he was superseded as architect at Buckingham Palace by James Pennethorne and at Windsor by Anthony Salvin. From the moment of her marriage to Prince Albert of Saxe-Coburg-Gotha in 1841, the Queen had tended to defer to him on artistic and architectural matters, and much that was achieved at Windsor during the 1840s and 1850s was their joint effort. The Queen had first met the Prince at Windsor when he visited the Castle in 1839 and had immediately fallen in love with him.

At Windsor Prince Albert took a keen interest in the restoration of the Lower Ward. This area had not formed part of Wyatville's great reconstruction scheme. Many of the towers, for instance, were in near-ruinous condition, and the subsidiary buildings were a patchwork of medieval masonry and Georgian brickwork. The aim was to repair it all, and to restore a consistent medieval character to the Lower Ward. Salvin was taken on to do this on Prince Albert's recommendation: 'The only man whose name occurred to the Prince as being likely to do this well was ... Mr Salvin.' Salvin was given instructions directly by Prince Albert. His letters frequently

JOSEPH NASH: *QUEEN VICTORIA AND PRINCE ALBERT HAVING BREAKFAST IN THE WHITE DRAWING ROOM AT WINDSOR IN 1848.*

SIR EDWIN LANDSEER: WINDSOR
CASTLE IN MODERN TIMES,
1841–5. Queen Victoria, Prince
Albert, Victoria The Princess Royal
(and some dogs and game) at
Windsor Castle.

refer to meetings with the Prince Consort to discuss the Windsor
works. In April 1857 he attended the Prince at Buckingham Palace,
and in April 1860 he met him at Windsor, noting, later in the same
year, 'the Prince Consort presses for the completion of the Lodge at
the foot of the Hundred Steps.' Salvin came to the Prince Consort's
attention through his work at the Tower of London, but had already
made his reputation as a castle expert with the construction of a
completely new one, Peckforton, in Cheshire (1844), for Lord
Tollemache and the restoration of many old ones, including Alnwick
in Northumberland, for the Duke of Northumberland.

The Hundred Steps were Salvin's first job at the Castle. The steps
are situated on the north side of St George's Chapel and lead from
the Canons' houses and cloisters down into the town. In the eighteenth century they were of brick with a wooden handrail. Salvin
rebuilt them in granite with a stone parapet. This part of the work
was completed in 1862, including the repair of the outer curtain wall
north of the Canons' houses. Salvin generally removed obtrusive
gables and medievalized the chimneys of the buildings in the Lower
Ward, as well as replacing Georgian sashes with cusped lancets and
mullion windows. The Garter Tower was repaired as a residence for
the Master of the Household. Crane's Building, a charming mid-
seventeenth-century range along the inner west wall of the Lower
Ward, was demolished and replaced by a new Guardhouse in toy-
fort style. The north-west tower of the Lower Ward, the Curfew
Tower, was reconstructed in 1862 with a tall candle-snuffer roof,
closer in spirit to Viollet-le-Duc's contemporary work on the fortifications at Carcasonne in the south of France than anything at

medieval Windsor. Salvin had seen Viollet-le-Duc's plans for the restoration of Carcassone, including the Tour du Trésor, the prototype of the Curfew Tower, at the Exposition Universelle at Paris in 1855. Prince Albert may also have suggested Viollet-le-Duc's work as a suitable source of inspiration for the Curfew Tower.

Salvin produced designs for rebuilding the Horseshoe Cloisters at the west end of St George's Chapel, but his plans for these were not adopted and the sweeping restoration of this picturesque group of brick and timber houses of the lay clerks or Vicars-choral was not carried out till 1871, and then under the direction of Sir George Gilbert Scott.

The end result of Prince Albert's and Salvin's campaign in the Lower Ward was to transform a venerable hotchpotch of ancient fragments and newer buildings into a more consistently Gothic composition. Unlike Wyatville's work in the Upper Ward, which is frankly late-Georgian Picturesque, a grand palace in Gothic dress, Salvin's work in the Lower Ward was executed with more scholarly attention, working from authentic models and fragments. A comparison of the Upper and Lower Wards underlines the difference between the serious Victorian Gothic Revival and more Picturesque late-Georgian architectural scene-making. It is rare to be able to judge both approaches side by side in the same building. Not everybody at the time or since was entirely happy. The lawyer Henry Vincent, a friend of Salvin's, wrote to another friend, Ralph Sneyd of Keele Hall, Staffordshire, in November 1858:

What in the world is Salvin doing at Windsor? I believe something to be necessary, – where the old Hill houses have been pulled down; but the less he does the better, I even wish (don't smite me) that they wouldn't meddle with your old Wooden Clocktower on top of the big stone one; – of course they will & I suppose must. – I have no opinion of P. Albert's taste; – I must go and see after him.

If the Prince Consort's taste was (posthumously) impressed heavily on the Lower Ward, he found an even more satisfying outlet for his enthusiasms in the grounds and parks. His interests in improving art, industry and the condition of the 'labouring classes' all found a perfect expression in agriculture at Windsor when he was appointed Ranger of the Great Park by Queen Victoria. He was also responsible for great improvements at the Queen's two private residences, Osborne House, the new holiday retreat constructed by them on the

Isle of Wight, and Balmoral Castle in Scotland, draining and making new roads, planting, fencing, and erecting model farm buildings and new cottages. It was at Windsor, however, that he was able to improve on the largest scale. He moulded the Home Park, the smaller park including Frogmore, next to the Castle, into one continuous estate by combining the grounds of Frogmore and the adjoining Shaw Farm, and by diverting the public road to Datchet when the railway was built. Magnificent new farm buildings were put up at Shaw Farm in 1853 in a grand Italianate style to the design of A.G. Dean, the leading farm architect of the day responsible for, among other things, the buildings at Longlands and the Model Farm at Holkham in Norfolk. The Home or Dairy Farm at Frogmore was also rebuilt in 1852 in a vague 'Tudorbethan' style to the design of J.R. Turnbull (Clerk of the Works at Windsor Castle), and six years later Prince Albert rebuilt George III's Dairy, which had various practical defects, to Turnbull's design in what was called the 'Renaissance style'.

The chief interest of the Dairy is its interior, which is a perfect demonstration of the 'art-manufactures' which Prince Albert was so keen on promoting. All the interior decoration was designed by John Thomas, Prince Albert's favourite sculptor/architect. The walls are completely covered with green and white Minton tiles and embellished with Minton's majolica bas-reliefs, while at either end are majolica fountains designed by Thomas. The brightly painted roof is supported on six ornamental columns. The whole ensemble is the finest Victorian dairy interior in England and far outshines, as it was intended to, any of the country-house dairies which Queen Victoria and the Prince had visited on their tours of England and Scotland in the 1840s, such as those at Arundel Castle in Sussex and Taymouth Castle in Perthshire.

New walled kitchen gardens and nurseries extending to 60 acres (24.2 ha), with enormous iron-framed greenhouses, were built at Frogmore at the same time, the greenhouses manufactured by Jones & Clarke. This followed the decision to consolidate the royal gardens at Windsor, and the sale of the old kitchen gardens at Kensington Palace for leasehold building development by the Crown Estate.

In the Great Park, the Prince initiated a programme of rejuvenation of the Long Walk, replacing decayed or stunted elms with new trees, and also provided large numbers of new estate cottages, mainly designed by S.S. Teulon. The Prince was a keen promoter

THE ROYAL DAIRY, FROGMORE:
detail of the stained-glass windows.

of good housing and embarked on a scheme at Windsor intended to ensure that every labourer on the royal estate was comfortably housed within one mile of his work. He also replaced George III's farm buildings at the Flemish Farm with a large new steading designed by J.R. Turnbull, though the Georgian timber buildings at the Norfolk Farm were retained and repaired. On the strength of his work at Windsor, the Prince was elected President of the Royal Agricultural Society.

Inside the Castle, the Prince Consort and Queen Victoria rearranged the hang of the pictures, drawing on the collections formed by the Stuarts, George III and Frederick, Prince of Wales, and above all George IV. It was the Prince Consort's idea to concentrate the large Rubens pictures in the King's Drawing Room, which was renamed the Rubens Room, the Van Dycks in the Queen's Ballroom which was renamed the Van Dyck Room, and the sixteenth-century portraits, including a group of Holbeins, in the Queen's Drawing Room, which was henceforth known as the

THE ROYAL DAIRY, FROGMORE:
detail showing the Minton tiles.

round the room. The Queen usually went to bed at 11 p.m., and the ladies went then, too; but the men could, if they wished, go to the billiards room on the ground floor at the west end of the north wing where they were allowed to smoke. This room was so far away that stories were told of guests who could not find their way back again in the dark and had to spend the night on a sofa in the state rooms. Queen Victoria disapproved of gaslight and the chandeliers in the Castle were lit by beeswax candles, though electric light was introduced at the end of her reign. She disliked the smell of coal fires and only beech logs were burnt in the fireplaces. She did not, however, require a high temperature and guests shivered as she sat happily in lukewarm rooms surrounded by healthy draughts from open windows – very different from the hothouse atmosphere that pervaded the rooms in George IV's time, when the King liked to sit in great heat, sipping cherry brandy and talking non-stop about a range of topics including how he was present at Waterloo ('So Your Majesty has often told me', the Duke of Wellington would reply).

Guests and household spent much of their time standing around, occasionally leaning surreptitiously against a wall to take some of the strain off their feet. Charles Greville, courtier and diarist, complained in 1838:

> the Court is not gay, but it is perhaps impossible that any Court should be gay where there is no social equality; where some ceremony, and a continual air of deference and respect must be observed, there can be no ease, and without ease there can be no real pleasure ... very little is done in common, and in this respect Windsor is totally unlike any other place. There is none of the sociability which makes the agreeableness of an English country house; there is no room in which the guests assemble, sit, lounge, and talk as they please and when they please; there is a billiard table, but in such a remote corner of the Castle that it might as well be in the town of Windsor; and there is a library well stocked with books, but hardly accessible, imperfectly warmed and only tenanted by the librarian.

The great ceremonial features of life at the Castle in Queen Victoria's time were the state visits of foreign monarchs. These were a new development in the nineteenth century, resulting from improved communication by railway and steam ship. The apartments in the Upper Ward could accommodate over 100 guests with ease. Throughout Queen Victoria's reign there was a succession of foreign visitors. The King of Prussia and other royal guests stayed for the christening of the Prince of Wales in 1842. The Emperor of Russia, King of Saxony and King Louis Philippe of France all came at different times in 1844. The Emperor Napoleon III and Empress Eugénie came in 1855; the Shah of Persia in 1873, Kaiser Wilhelm II of Germany and the Emir of Afghanistan in 1895. A particularly exotic visit was that of a deputation from Siam in 1858 in which the emissaries crept on all fours along the carpet of the Garter Throne Room, as was their custom, nearly reducing the Queen to giggles: 'Really, it was most difficult to keep one's countenance', she noted in her diary.

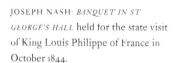

JOSEPH NASH: *BANQUET IN ST GEORGE'S HALL* held for the state visit of King Louis Philippe of France in October 1844.

THE KING'S BED CHAMBER, as redecorated for the state visit of Napoleon III in 1855. The bed, which had been George IV's, remains in the room today and retains its green and purple Napoleonic hangings.

The great feature of these state visits was a banquet in St George's Hall, which was elaborately decked for the occasion with George IV's incomparable gold plate and flowers from the hothouses at Frogmore. Several of the visiting monarchs, including King Louis Philippe, King Victor Emmanuel I of Italy, Napoleon III and Kaiser Wilhelm II were invested with the Garter by the Queen at special installation ceremonies in the Garter Throne Room.

EDWARD MATTHEW WARD: *THE INVESTITURE OF NAPOLEON III WITH THE ORDER OF THE GARTER, 18 APRIL 1855*, 1860. The visit to Windsor of Napoleon III of France and the Empress Eugénie in 1855 was one of a number of splendid state visits organized at the Castle in Queen Victoria's reign.

For Napoleon III's visit in 1855 the state rooms were partially redecorated by Crace. George IV's domed and plumed bed, attributed to Jacob, from Carlton House, was moved to the King's Bed Chamber, rehung in the Napoleonic colours of green and purple, and trimmed with Mrs Pawsey's needlework, probably taken from George III's old throne canopy. The bed still remains in this position and this condition. The Waterloo Chamber was also redecorated by Crace in an idiosyncratic Tudorbethan manner, but with handsome glass chandeliers by Osler.

As well as these great formal state occasions, there were more social events including dances, concerts, operas and plays. Small dances were held in the Crimson Drawing Room, and plays in the King's Drawing Room with a stage rigged up in the bay window. Larger events took place in the Waterloo Chamber, which was also used (after the great Duke of Wellington's death) for the annual Waterloo banquet in June. Another innovation at Windsor was the Christmas party and the Christmas tree with a display of family Christmas presents, which continued on a larger scale the German tradition introduced by Queen Charlotte.

The tenor of royal life at Windsor was broken by the sudden and premature death of Prince Albert. He died of typhoid fever at Windsor Castle on 14 December 1861, plunging Queen Victoria into

JAMES ROBERTS: WATERCOLOUR OF THE QUEEN'S CHRISTMAS TREE AT WINDSOR CASTLE in 1850. Christmas was a great feature of Victorian Windsor. The German custom of a Christmas tree is reputed to have been brought to England by Queen Charlotte, wife of George III.

WILLIAM CORDEN: WATERCOLOUR
OF THE BLUE ROOM where the
Prince Consort died on 14 December
1861. Queen Victoria kept the room as
it was at the time of the Prince's
death for the rest of her life.

grief-stricken widowhood. The Queen was with him at the end. She wrote in her diary: 'I stood up, kissed his dear heavenly forehead and called out in a bitter and agonising cry "Oh! my dear Darling" and then dropped on my knees in mute, distracted despair.' The Walter Scott novel which the Prince had been reading was put in the Royal Library by the Queen with an inscription marking the place he had reached when he died. It is still there.

After his death a sombre atmosphere permeated the Castle and there was constantly the feeling that somebody was missing. In the manner of German mourning, his rooms were left exactly as they were at the time of his death; fresh water was placed on the wash-stand daily, and his clothes were brushed ready for use. The ceiling was painted in Raphaelesque colours with angels and stars by Professor Gruner.

The late Victorian architectural history of Windsor is largely that of the intermittent construction of suitable memorials to Prince Albert. The chapel over the Tomb House was converted by the Queen into a glowing shrine to his memory, the Albert Memorial Chapel. The interior was stunningly remodelled from 1863 to 1873 by Sir Gilbert Scott and Baron H. de Triqueti; the walls were lined with etched marble reliefs of biblical subjects by Jules Destréez, the vaults encrusted with gold mosaic by Antonio Salviati, and the windows filled with stained glass by Clayton & Bell. There is nothing else like this in England, though there are parallels in France and Germany. It is rich, restrained and deeply moving. As well as this cenotaph chapel, Queen Victoria erected a mausoleum for her

ALBERT MEMORIAL CHAPEL: detail of Victorian decoration.

THE ALBERT MEMORIAL CHAPEL. The old Tombhouse, occupying the shell of the Lady Chapel of St George's Chapel, was restored and richly decorated by Queen Victoria in 1863 as a memorial to Prince Albert. The gold mosaic which encrusts the vaults was by Antonio Salviati.

husband and herself at Frogmore. This was perhaps the most novel of the architectural changes initiated in her reign by the Queen. Hitherto the sovereigns of this country had been buried in ancient churches with royal associations. The Queen's immediate forerunners had been buried at St George's Chapel. For herself and her husband, however, the Queen preferred to build a special tomb house in a private garden. Her decision was not the direct consequence of her husband's premature death, but the realization of a long-meditated plan which owed its origins to the Saxe-Coburg family from which both her mother and her husband came. Her uncle, Leopold of Saxe-Coburg (later King of the Belgians), had, following the death of his wife Princess Charlotte, the only daughter of George IV, built a small Gothic mausoleum in the grounds of Claremont, Surrey, and this gave Queen Victoria and Prince Albert the idea of building a mausoleum for themselves. In 1844 the Prince and his brothers erected such a mausoleum at Coburg for their father and his family. Queen Victoria's mother asked if she could be buried in a mausoleum at Coburg too. This was impractical, and so, instead, a mausoleum was built for her in the grounds of Frogmore, where she had lived since 1841: it comprised a rotunda of Penrhyn granite, designed by Ludwig Gruner and executed by A.J. Humbert from 1860, which formed an overture for the main royal mausoleum.

THE ROYAL MAUSOLEUM, Frogmore: detail of the interior showing Ludwig Gruner's Italianate painted decoration.

LUDWIG GRUNER: DESIGN FOR THE
ROYAL MAUSOLEUM AT
FROGMORE, commissioned by
Queen Victoria in 1863 for Prince
Albert and herself. The tragedy of
the Prince's death at Windsor Castle
in 1861 overshadowed the remaining
forty years of the Queen's reign.

Following the death of the Prince Consort, Queen Victoria lost no
time in carrying into effect her ideas for the royal mausoleum and
chose a site for it close to her mother's at Frogmore. She employed
the Prince's architects – Gruner to make the designs and Humbert to
carry them out – in the years 1862-71. The exterior is Lombardic, the
walls of granite and Portland stone. The roof is sheathed in
Australian copper. Richly cast gun-metal doors give access to the
splendid spectacle of the interior, which is in the richest Italian High

Renaissance style, embellished with marble and stencilled paintwork of red, dark blue and yellow. Round the walls are frescoes by German and Italian artists in the manner of Raphael, whom the Prince Consort had thought the greatest of all artists. Under the central dome is a sarcophagus of marble, bronze and flawless Aberdeen granite, with glistening white effigies of Prince Albert and Queen Victoria by Baron Marochetti. The Queen's was executed at the same time as the Prince's and kept in store till her death in 1901, by which time it was so long since it had been made that there was some difficulty remembering where it was. Though executed after his death, the Royal Mausoleum at Frogmore is the finest expression of Prince Albert's personal taste, just as the Queen intended it to be. Though comparatively small in scale, it is among the two or three finest examples in Europe of mid-nineteenth-century Classical taste, comparable with Von Klenze's Hermitage extension in St Petersburg or St Paul's Outside the Walls in Rome. 'The Queen's grief still sobs through its interior as though she had left her sorrow on earth to haunt this rich, forbidding temple to her loneliness.'

CARLO MAROCHETTI: WHITE MARBLE EFFIGIES OF QUEEN VICTORIA AND PRINCE ALBERT in the Royal Mausoleum at Windsor.

CHAPTER SIX

THE TWENTIETH CENTURY

For the greater part of the twentieth century Windsor Castle survived much as it had been created and used in the nineteenth century. Edward VII, after he came to the throne in 1901, reacted against the rather sombre and cluttered character which the interior of the Castle had acquired during the latter part of Queen Victoria's reign. He caused many of the rooms in the Castle to be rearranged and redecorated, as well as generally modernizing the Upper Ward, extending the electric light, and introducing central heating and new bathrooms. In the King's own private apartments in the east range he hung the walls of the rooms with green damask and installed a magnificent new bathroom fitted up in white and green cippolino marble. In Queen Alexandra's rooms in the Victoria Tower the walls of her bedroom were hung with pink satin, and her bathroom was lined with pink-and-white marble.

In the State Apartments, too, an attempt was made to lighten the character of the nineteenth-century decorations. In particular, the armour in the Grand Staircase, Grand Vestibule, Guard Chamber and St George's Hall was thinned out and rearranged, partly to make room for some additions of the King's own. In the Guard Chamber, these changes involved the removal of the upper tier of oak wainscot, designed by Wyatville, Bernasconi's plaster statues in niches and the carved overmantel. The chief addition here was the magnificent equestrian figure with the armour of the King's Champion, made at Greenwich in 1585 and supposed to have been used at the Coronation banquet of George I and George II. It was presented to Edward VII in 1901 by a group of friends including Sir Ernest Cassel, the celebrated financier.

The state rooms were hung *en suite* with crimson damask, and

SIR JAMES GUNN: *STATE PORTRAIT OF QUEEN ELIZABETH II*, 1954–6, wearing Coronation robes. It hangs in the Garter Throne Room at Windsor Castle.

THE FUNERAL PROCESSION OF
KING GEORGE VI AT WINDSOR
CASTLE in 1952.

During the present reign Windsor Castle has been the principal home of the royal family, The Queen and her sister Princess Margaret having spent most of their childhood there during the Second World War. The Court is officially in residence in April and during Ascot Week in June when the annual Garter Day celebrations take place with the installation of new Knights, lunch in the Waterloo Chamber and a choral service in St George's Chapel. The present Garter Service was revived by King George VI in 1947. The Castle has also seen several splendid recent state and private visits, including those of President Reagan of the United States and President Lech Walesa of Poland. The Queen and her family spend most of their private weekends at the Castle and, until recent building work interrupted the traditional routine, Christmas was always spent there. A distinctive feature of hospitality at Windsor Castle is still the invitation to 'dine and sleep' which goes back to Queen Victoria's time and encompasses people prominent in many walks of life as well as the Queen's ministers.

On 20 November 1992 a serious fire broke out in the Queen's Private Chapel at the north-east angle of the Upper Ward. It is thought to have been caused by a spotlight igniting a curtain high above the altar. Despite the efforts of the Castle staff and the fire brigade, the fire spread rapidly at roof level, destroying the ceilings of George IV's St George's Hall and Grand Reception Room as well as gutting the Private Chapel, State Dining Room, Brunswick Tower, Crimson Drawing Room and various subsidiary and service rooms in the north-east corner of the Castle. By great good fortune the rooms worst affected by the fire were empty at the time as they were in

THE STATE VISIT OF PRESIDENT
LECH WALESA OF POLAND TO
WINDSOR CASTLE in April 1991.

THE FIRE IN THE UPPER WARD AT WINDSOR CASTLE, 1992.

ST GEORGE'S HALL before and after the destruction of the roof by fire in 1992.

JOHN PIPER: *THE QUADRANGLE OF THE UPPER WARD FROM THE ROUND TOWER*. Commissioned by King George VI and Queen Elizabeth.

course of being rewired. As a result, miraculously few of the Castle's artistic treasures were destroyed. The principal casualties were a Pugin sideboard and a portrait of George III by Sir William Beechey, both in the Dining Room, which were too big to move.

The work of repair began immediately after the fire. Already the shell of the damaged portion has been made weather-tight with a new roof and windows, and work is proceeding rapidly on the interior. George IV's damaged rooms will be reinstated exactly as they were, but the Chapel area is to be redesigned, and a new, more impressive timber ceiling is being devised for St George's Hall.

Two committees were set up to advise on the restoration of the fire-damaged areas. The principal, the Windsor Castle Restoration Committee chaired by the Duke of Edinburgh, was in overall control of the restoration project and the other committee chaired by the Prince of Wales, known as the Windsor Castle Restoration Design Committee, had a more specific role to prepare the design briefs and a shortlist of prospective designers, and to recommend the best architect to redesign those parts worst affected, by creating a new tribune in the area formerly occupied by the Private Chapel, as well as a new ceiling for St George's Hall.

The Crown Buildings Group of English Heritage carried out

extensive archaeological investigation of the fire-damaged areas, sifting through the rubble and salvaging pieces which were capable of being reused in the restoration work, as well as investigating the ancient fabric for new information about the historical evolution of the buildings, in those places which had been opened up by the fire. English Heritage has also advised on the specifically historic buildings aspects of the restoration.

Donald Insall & Partners, one of the leading firms of specialist conservation architects in the country, were awarded the contracts for the restoration of those parts of the Castle which had been damaged but not totally destroyed by the fire. This included the Great Kitchen, where the medieval roof structure, despite some charring of timbers, had survived the flames and is being repaired to its pre-fire appearance; the Grand Reception Room where the wall decorations survived the fire unscathed; and Bernasconi's elaborate ceiling, which is capable of being recreated from fragments rescued from the debris. The Green Drawing Room was only slightly damaged in the fire and is being repaired. The Crimson Drawing Room was more seriously affected, and the magnificent carved door panels were badly charred. The damaged parts are being recarved. The State Dining Room, in the Prince of Wales Tower, and the Octagon Dining Room in the Brunswick Tower, were both gutted, but their Wyatville chimneypieces, windows and proportions survived, as did most of Pugin's furniture. Rebuilding these rooms to new designs was considered, and various modern schemes were proposed and examined; but none of them was thought to be an improvement on their former character. So it was decided, after careful deliberation, to restore these as well to their original Wyatville appearance.

All the service areas round the kitchen yard in the north-east corner of the building and the staff bedrooms on the upper floors which were destroyed in the fire are being replanned and rebuilt to modern standards. As well as the functional improvements which this will allow, these works have also enabled some of Edward III's medieval fabric in the Kitchen Court to be cleared of miscellaneous later accretions and restored to view.

The area most seriously damaged by the fire was Blore's Private Chapel, the Holbein and Stuart Rooms, and the east end and roof of St George's Hall. Nothing remains of the Chapel apart from the reredos and window tracery above it. The carved oak screen and two-sided Willis organ, built for Queen Victoria, between the

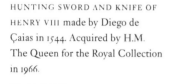

HUNTING SWORD AND KNIFE OF HENRY VIII made by Diego de Çaias in 1544. Acquired by H.M. The Queen for the Royal Collection in 1966.

ASTRONOMICAL CLOCK BY JOHN PYKE IN A LACQUERED CASE, c. 1750. Purchased by H.M. The Queen for the Royal Collection in 1960.

QUEEN CHARLOTTE'S JEWEL
CABINET, made by Vile & Cobb
in 1762. One of a series of items
with royal connections which were
reacquired by Queen Mary for the
Royal Collection.

Chapel and St George's Hall were totally destroyed. Though a
tragic loss, this has presented the opportunity to improve the
communications in this part of the Castle and to restore the processional link between St George's Hall and the Grand Corridor and
royal apartments, which had been severed by Queen Victoria's
conversion of the Band Room to a Chapel.

The architects chosen from a shortlist of four – just as George
IV chose an architect in 1824 – were the Sidell Gibson Partnership.
The Sidell Gibson Partnership has been responsible for a number of
prominent new buildings in London, including Grand Buildings in
Trafalgar Square, and the new Jewel House at the Tower of London,
but was chosen for the work at Windsor on the strength of their
proposed plans and feeling for the Gothic style. The rebuilt area
will include a new, smaller private chapel ingeniously tucked into
the space formerly occupied by the Holbein and Stuart Rooms, and
the contrivance of a new octagonal tribune on the site of the main
body of the old chapel. One side wall comprises the surviving stone

ST GEORGE'S HALL PERSPECTIVE.
New design for the ceiling by
Giles Downes of the Sidell Gibson
Partnership

reredos panelling and traceried altar window. The octagon neatly turns the axis between the Grand Corridor and St George's Hall. The tribune is two storeys high, with an intermediate balcony supported on clustered timber columns, and a modern star-vaulted timber roof with a central polygonal cupola. It derives its general inspiration from the medieval octagons at Ely Cathedral and the abbey of Batalha in Portugal, which was James Wyatt's source for his short-lived Gothic masterpiece at Fonthill Abbey in Wiltshire. But all the detail, while Gothic in inspiration, is original and not derived from historical sources. The tribune, as well as being a processional space, will be used for the display of works of art from the Royal Collection.

In St George's Hall, Jeffry Wyatville's ceiling, which appeared to be of timber, was in fact plasterwork by Bernasconi, painted to resemble oak graining. Its very shallow pitch exacerbated the unsatisfactory proportions of the room. The opportunity has therefore been taken to construct a new ceiling, in the form of a modern hammerbeam roof of English oak. All the heraldic decorations, with the shields of the Knights of the Garter from the foundation of the Order, will be reinstated as before. The destroyed screen at the east end of the Hall is being replaced with a new design. The wall panelling, western screen and gallery, and the contents, including trophies of armour, all survived the fire and will be retained as they were.

Both the restored rooms and the newly designed work at Windsor have offered an excellent opportunity for modern craftsmanship, enabling the current generation to pitch its skills against the glories of Caroline and Regency craftsmanship. The contract is due to be completed by 1998; the work is being funded entirely from the visitor income earned at Windsor Castle and Buckingham Palace, with no extra contribution by the tax-payer.

Though very destructive and shocking at the time, the fire was less disastrous than originally thought. The damage to the Royal Collection was minimal. The reconstruction of the damaged area has allowed scope for many improvements both to the functioning of the domestic side, and in the decoration of the damaged rooms. The fire has provided opportunities for the patronage of modern Gothic architecture and craftsmanship, as well as the uncovering and restoration of some of the fabric of Edward III's medieval Windsor, for so long concealed by later work. The Upper Ward retains its place among the greatest European palaces, where an incomparable assemblage of works of art is still displayed as a living, historic entity in the settings specially designed for the purpose and as a backdrop to court ceremonial and royal family life.